Grill Cookbook

2000 Days of Super Easy & Delicious Grill Recipes with a 30-Day Meal Plan for Creating Flavorful and Memorable Meals

Enjoy Nutritious Meals with Unmatched Flavor

Barry Vesper

Legal & Disclaimer

The content and information contained in this book has been compiled from reliable sources, which are accurate based on the knowledge, belief, expertise and information of the Author. The author cannot be held liable for any omissions and/or errors.

TABLE OF CONTENTS

INTRODUCTION..................................7
CHAPTER 1: INTRODUCTION TO GRILLING.. 8
  Welcome to the World of Grilling and Smoking................................. 8
  Choosing The Right Equipment................... 8
  Essential Tools And Accessories.................9
  Understanding Heat And Temperature........10
  Preparing Your Ingredients.........................12
  Troubleshooting And Tips.........................14
CHAPTER 2: 30-DAY MEAL PLAN................. 17
CHAPTER 3: BREAKFASTS:.................. 20
Classic Grilled Morning Feasts....................20
    Grilled Bacon and Egg Breakfast Sandwich................................. 20
    Grilled Sausage and Hash Browns.......20
    Grilled Mushroom and Spinach Frittata. 21
    Grilled Breakfast Burrito with Eggs and Chorizo.......................... 21
    Grilled Breakfast Flatbread with Eggs and Bacon................................. 22
    Grilled Breakfast Casserole with Sausage and Eggs........................ 22
CHAPTER 4: BREAKFAST: Flavorful Taco and Quesadilla Creations....................................22
    Grilled Breakfast Quesadilla with Bacon and Cheese.......................... 23
    Grilled Breakfast Tacos with Chorizo and Eggs.............................. 23
    Grilled Chicken and Black Bean Quesadillas..............................24
    Grilled Chicken and Black Bean Quesadillas..............................24
    Grilled Shrimp and Egg Tacos with Lime Crema..............................25
    Grilled Pork Sausage and Egg Tacos....25
    Grilled Spicy Breakfast Tacos with Jalapeños..............................26
    Grilled Mushroom and Spinach Quesadillas..............................26
    Grilled Corn and Zucchini Quesadillas.. 27
    Bacon and Egg Salad..........................27
CHAPTER 5: BREAKFASTS: Energizing Protein-Powered Breakfasts......................... 28
    Grilled Breakfast Skewers with Sausage and Veggies..............................28
    Grilled Cinnamon Rolls with Cream Cheese Icing..............................28
    Grilled Greek Salad with Grilled Chicken and Feta.............................. 29
    Grilled Lentil and Quinoa Breakfast Bowl.. 29
CHAPTER 6: BREAKFAST: Indulgent Weekend Brunch Inspirations.......................30
    Grilled Breakfast Pizza with Eggs and Sausage.............................. 30
    Grilled Pancakes with Maple Syrup and Fresh Berries.............................. 30
    Grilled English Muffin............................31
    Casserole with grilled vegetables and feta for breakfast..............................31
CHAPTER 7: LUNCHES: Delectable Burger and Sandwich Delights.................................32
    Classic Grilled Cheeseburger...............32
    BBQ Bacon Cheeseburger....................32
    Grilled Portobello Mushroom Burger with Swiss Cheese.......................................33
    Spicy Jalapeño Burger with Pepper Jack Cheese.............................. 33
    Grilled Chicken Club Sandwich with Avocado..............................34
    Turkey Burger with Cranberry Sauce.... 34
CHAPTER 8: LUNCHES: Steaks....................35
    Grilled Ribeye Steak with Garlic Butter and Rosemary Potatoes.......................35
    Grilled Flank Steak with Soy-Ginger Marinade and Sesame Green Beans.... 35
    Grilled Sirloin Steak with Chimichurri Sauce and Grilled Asparagus................36
    Grilled T-Bone Steak with Herb Butter and Creamed Spinach..............................36
    Grilled Filet Mignon with Blue Cheese Butter and Mashed Cauliflower............. 37
    Grilled New York Strip with Balsamic Glaze and Roasted Brussels Sprouts....37
CHAPTER 9: LUNCHES: Ribs.................... 38
    Grilled Baby Back Ribs with BBQ Sauce and Coleslaw.......................................38
    Grilled Spare Ribs with Sweet and Spicy

Glaze and Baked Beans......................38

Grilled Country Style Ribs with Mustard Sauce and Potato Salad......................39

Grilled Beef Short Ribs with Red Wine Sauce and Garlic Mashed Potatoes......39

CHAPTER 10: LUNCHES: Chicken............. 40

Grilled BBQ Chicken Thighs with Corn on the Cob..................40

Grilled Chicken Wings with Buffalo Sauce and Celery Sticks..................40

Grilled Lemon Herb Chicken Breasts with Quinoa Salad..................41

Grilled Honey Mustard Chicken Drumsticks with Sweet Potato Fries......41

CHAPTER 11: LUNCHES: Turkey..................42

Grilled Spicy Turkey Sausage with Bell Peppers and Onions..................42

Grilled Turkey Thighs with Garlic and Rosemary and Roasted Carrots...........42

Grilled Turkey Breast with Herb Marinade and Wild Rice Pilaf.................. 43

Grilled BBQ Turkey Legs with Macaroni and Cheese.................. 43

Grilled Turkey Meatballs with Spaghetti Squash.................. 44

Grilled Turkey Kabobs with Veggies and Couscous..................44

CHAPTER 12: LUNCHES: Pork..................45

Grilled Pork Chops with Apple Glaze and Sautéed Spinach.................. 45

Grilled Pork Tenderloin with Herb Rub and Roasted Sweet Potatoes..............45

Grilled BBQ Pulled Pork with Coleslaw and Cornbread..................46

Grilled Pork Belly with Honey Soy Glaze and Stir-Fried Vegetables..................46

Grilled Pork Sausages with Onions and German Potato Salad..................47

Grilled Pork Loin with Mustard Sauce and Green Bean Almondine..................47

CHAPTER 13: LUNCHES: Beef..................48

Grilled Pork Chops with Apple Glaze and Sautéed Spinach.................. 48

Grilled Beef Tenderloin with Garlic and Herb Roasted Potatoes.................. 48

Grilled Beef and Veggie Stir-Fry with Jasmine Rice..................49

Grilled Teriyaki Beef with Steamed

Broccoli and Rice Noodles.................... 49

CHAPTER 14: SNACK: Appetizers............... 50

Grilled Stuffed Jalapeños with Cream Cheese..................50

Grilled Artichoke Hearts with Lemon Aioli. 50

Grilled Avocado Halves with Salsa........51

Grilled Halloumi Cheese with Lemon.... 51

CHAPTER 15: SNACK: Dips and Spreads.... 52

Smoky Grilled Eggplant Dip..................52

Grilled Artichoke Spinach Dip...............52

Grilled Avocado and Mango Salsa........ 53

Grilled Jalapeño and Lime Hummus..... 53

CHAPTER 16: DESSERTS: Quick and Easy Dessert Ideas..................54

Grilled Lemon Pound Cake with Berries54

Grilled Pear and Blue Cheese Spread.. 54

Grilled Blueberry Crisp.................. 55

Grilled Coconut Macaroons..................55

Grilled Pumpkin Pie Slices.................. 56

Grilled Cheesecake with Berry Compote... 56

CHAPTER 17: DINNER: Low Fat & Low Calorie Options..................57

Grilled Lemon Herb Chicken Breasts with Steamed Broccoli.................. 57

Grilled Turkey Burgers with Spinach and Feta.................. 57

Grilled Chicken and Vegetable Skewers with Quinoa..................58

Grilled Portobello Mushrooms with Garlic and Thyme..................58

Grilled Zucchini Boats with Lean Turkey and Marinara.................. 59

Grilled Eggplant Parmesan with Fresh Basil..................59

Grilled Cod Fillet with Lemon Dill Sauce and Asparagus..................... 60

Grilled Chicken Caesar Salad with Light Dressing.................. 60

Grilled Tilapia with Mango Salsa and Wild Rice.................. 61

Grilled Eggplant and Tomato Stack....... 61

CHAPTER 18: DINNER: Hearty Salads with Grilled Proteins..................62

Grilled Pork Tenderloin Salad with Apples and Pecans..................62

Grilled Halloumi and Watermelon Salad 62

Grilled Greek Chicken Salad with Tzatziki. 63

Grilled Turkey and Cranberry Salad...... 63

Grilled Flank Steak and Arugula Salad ..64

Grilled BBQ Chicken Salad with Corn and Black Beans...64

CHAPTER 19: DINNER: Grilled Vegetables and Plant-Based Dishes................................. 65

Grilled Cauliflower Steaks with Romesco Sauce.. 65

Grilled Ratatouille................................. 65

Grilled Butternut Squash and Kale Salad.. 66

Grilled Zucchini Rolls with Goat Cheese... 66

Grilled Vegetable Wrap with Hummus...67

Grilled Stuffed Tomatoes with Rice and Herbs...67

CHAPTER 20: DINNER: Seafood Specialties 68

Grilled Salmon with Dill Yogurt Sauce... 68

Grilled Shrimp Skewers with Lemon Garlic Butter..68

Grilled Tuna Steaks with Avocado Salsa... 69

Grilled Swordfish with Pineapple Salsa. 69

CHAPTER 21: DINNER: Family-Style Dinner Ideas.. 70

Grilled Halibut with Tomato Basil Relish 70

Grilled Mahi-Mahi Tacos with Mango Slaw 70

Grilled Seafood Paella...........................71

Grilled Steak Fajitas with Guacamole....71

Grilled Vegetable Lasagna....................72

CHAPTER 22: BONUSES..............................73

Your Ultimate Grocery Shopping Guide...... 73

Grocery Shopping List for 7-Day Meal Plan.. 73

Grocery Shopping List for 8-14 Day Meal Plan.. 74

Grocery Shopping List for 15-21 Day Meal Plan...75

Grocery Shopping List for 22-28 Day Meal Plan...76

INTRODUCTION

Dear readers,

Barry Vesper, a renowned chef and aficionado of outdoor cooking, shares his grilling expertise in this comprehensive guide. This book is designed to help you relish the joys of outdoor feasts, whether during the summer or throughout the year.

Grilling offers a fantastic combination of ease, flexibility, and health benefits. The intense heat and open flames impart a unique char and smoky essence, making it ideal for everything from succulent burgers and steaks to tender fish and crispy vegetables. Grilling requires less oil, leading to healthier meals without sacrificing taste. Its capacity to cook various foods at once makes it perfect for family dinners and social gatherings.

Barry's recipes are a delightful blend of flavors, colors, and textures, expertly crafted to deliver quick, nutritious, and delectable meals. His commitment to making outdoor cooking accessible and enjoyable is evident in every dish. To kickstart your grilling adventure, Barry has included a 30-day meal plan, simplifying the process of planning and preparing balanced meals your whole family will enjoy. This meal plan encompasses a wide array of dishes rich in proteins, healthy fats, and carbohydrates, ensuring you maintain a nutritious diet while savoring delicious food.

With Barry Vesper as your mentor, your grilling journey will be both straightforward and enjoyable. His knowledge and passion will motivate you to create extraordinary meals, transforming every outdoor event into a culinary delight. Embrace the boundless possibilities of grilling and reap the rich flavors and health benefits it offers. Happy grilling!

CHAPTER 1: INTRODUCTION TO GRILLING

Welcome to the World of Grilling and Smoking

Welcome to the World of Grilling and Smoking Grilling and smoking are more than just cooking methods; they are a way of life. From backyard barbecues to family gatherings, these techniques bring people together, creating flavors that are both deep and memorable. Whether you are a beginner or looking to refine your skills, understanding the basics is the first step to mastering the art of grilling and smoking.

Benefits of Grilling and Smoking

Enhanced Flavor: The high heat of grilling caramelizes the natural sugars in food, creating a delicious char and depth of flavor. Smoking infuses food with a rich, smoky aroma that is unparalleled.

Healthier Cooking: Grilling allows fat to drip away from meat, reducing the overall fat content. Additionally, smoking can help preserve food naturally without the need for preservatives.

Versatility: From meats and seafood to vegetables and even fruits, the grill and smoker can handle it all. You can experiment with a wide range of ingredients and recipes.

Social Experience: Grilling and smoking are social activities that bring people together. Whether it's a weekend cookout or a holiday feast, these methods create a communal atmosphere.

Choosing The Right Equipment

Selecting the right equipment is crucial to mastering the art of grilling and smoking. With a variety of options available, making the right choice can seem overwhelming. This chapter will guide you through the different types of grills and smokers, as well as essential accessories, to help you make an informed decision that suits your needs and preferences.

Types of Grills

Charcoal Grills

Flavor: Charcoal grills are renowned for the rich, smoky flavor they impart to food. The charcoal provides a distinct taste that many grilling enthusiasts love.
Heat Control: These grills offer high heat for searing and low, indirect heat for slow cooking. Managing the heat requires skill and practice, as it involves adjusting the vents and charcoal placement.
Portability: Many charcoal grills are portable, making them a great option for camping trips and tailgating.

Gas Grills

Convenience: Gas grills are known for their ease of use. They heat up quickly and provide precise temperature control with the turn of a knob.
Cleanliness: Gas grills burn cleanly, reducing the amount of soot and ash compared to charcoal grills.
Versatility: With multiple burners, gas grills allow you to create different heat zones,

making it easier to cook various types of food simultaneously.

Electric Grills

Indoor Use: Electric grills are perfect for indoor cooking or for use in areas with restrictions on open flames.
Ease of Use: These grills are straightforward to operate, requiring only an electrical outlet to function.
Minimal Smoke: Electric grills produce less smoke, making them ideal for apartments and other confined spaces.

Pellet Grills

Flavor: Pellet grills use wood pellets as fuel, providing a unique smoky flavor similar to that of a charcoal grill.
Temperature Control: These grills offer precise temperature control, making them versatile for both grilling and smoking.
Automation: Many pellet grills come with automated features that maintain a consistent temperature, allowing for a more hands-off cooking experience.

Kamado Grills

Insulation: Kamado grills are made from thick ceramic material, which retains heat exceptionally well. This makes them versatile for grilling, smoking, and even baking.
Fuel Efficiency: These grills use less charcoal than traditional grills due to their excellent heat retention.
Temperature Range: Kamado grills can reach very high temperatures for searing or maintain low temperatures for slow cooking.

Essential Tools And Accessories

Grill Brush
Keeping your grill clean is essential for both flavor and safety. A good-quality grill brush helps remove food particles and residue from the grates.

Tongs and Spatula
Long-handled tongs and a sturdy spatula are necessary for handling food safely and efficiently. Look for tools with heat-resistant handles.

Meat Thermometer
Ensuring that your food is cooked to the proper temperature is crucial. A reliable meat thermometer helps you achieve perfect results every time.

Charcoal Chimney Starter
For those using charcoal grills, a chimney starter is an efficient way to light charcoal without the need for lighter fluid, resulting in a cleaner burn and better flavor.

Grill Cover
Protecting your grill from the elements prolongs its lifespan. Invest in a durable cover to shield your grill from rain, snow, and UV rays.

Drip Pans and Foil
Drip pans help catch grease and prevent flare-ups, while foil can be used for wrapping food or lining grates for easier cleanup.

Heat-Resistant Gloves
Handling hot grates, pans, and food requires proper protection. Heat-resistant gloves keep your hands safe from burns.

Skewers

Metal or bamboo skewers are perfect for grilling kabobs and making sure small pieces of food don't fall through the grates.

Basting Brush

A silicone basting brush is ideal for applying marinades and sauces evenly without shedding bristles.

Grill Basket

A grill basket is useful for cooking small

Understanding Heat And Temperature

Mastering heat and temperature is the cornerstone of successful grilling and smoking. Whether you're searing a steak to perfection or smoking a brisket for hours, knowing how to control and utilize heat is crucial. This chapter will delve into the fundamentals of heat management, helping you achieve consistent and delicious results every time you fire up your grill or smoker.

The Basics of Heat Transfer

Heat transfer is the process of heat moving from one place to another, and it occurs in three main ways: conduction, convection, and radiation.

Conduction: This is the direct transfer of heat through a solid object. When you place a steak on a hot grill grate, heat transfers from the metal to the meat through conduction.

Convection: This involves the transfer of heat through a fluid, such as air or water. In grilling, hot air circulates around the food, cooking it evenly. This is especially important in smoking, where low and slow cooking relies heavily on convection.

Radiation: This is the transfer of heat through electromagnetic waves. The glowing coals or flames beneath your grill emit radiant heat, which cooks the food above.

Direct vs. Indirect Cooking

Understanding the difference between direct and indirect cooking is essential for achieving the right results with different types of food.

Direct Cooking:

Method: Food is placed directly over the heat source.
Best For: Quick-cooking items like steaks, burgers, hot dogs, and vegetables.
Heat Level: High heat (400-550°F / 204-288°C) is typically used.
Advantages: Quick searing and charred flavor.

Indirect Cooking:

Method: Food is placed to the side of the heat source, not directly over it.
Best For: Larger cuts of meat like roasts, whole chickens, and ribs that require longer cooking times.
Heat Level: Lower, more controlled heat (225-300°F / 107-149°C).
Advantages: Gentle, even cooking that prevents burning and allows for better smoke absorption in smoking.

Creating Heat Zones

Creating distinct heat zones on your grill allows for greater flexibility and control, letting you cook different foods simultaneously or manage the cooking process more precisely.

Two-Zone Setup:

Direct Zone: High heat for searing.
Indirect Zone: Lower heat for slow cooking.
How-To: For charcoal grills, pile the coals on one side. For gas grills, light burners on one side only.

Three-Zone Setup:

High Heat Zone: For intense searing.
Medium Heat Zone: For finishing cooking.
Low Heat Zone: For keeping food warm or for slow cooking.
How-To: Adjust the coal placement or burner settings to create three distinct zones.

Controlling Temperature

Accurate temperature control is vital for both grilling and smoking. Here's how to manage it effectively:

Charcoal Grills:

Vent Adjustments: The intake vent controls oxygen flow to the coals, and the exhaust vent lets out heat and smoke. Open vents increase temperature, while closed vents decrease it.

Coal Arrangement: Spread coals for even heat or pile them for high heat zones.

Gas Grills:

Burner Control: Adjust the knobs to increase or decrease flame size. Use multiple burners to create heat zones.
Lid Position: Keeping the lid closed retains heat, while opening it reduces temperature quickly.

Smokers:

Water Pan: Using a water pan helps regulate temperature by stabilizing heat and adding moisture to the cooking environment.
Fuel Management: Add wood chips or chunks for smoke, and manage the fuel source to maintain a steady temperature.

Using a Meat Thermometer

A reliable meat thermometer is an indispensable tool for achieving perfectly cooked food. Here's how to use it effectively:

Instant-Read Thermometers: Provide quick temperature readings and are perfect for checking doneness of steaks, chops, and burgers.

Leave-In Thermometers: Ideal for large cuts of meat that cook slowly, like roasts and whole poultry. These can stay in the meat while it cooks, giving continuous temperature readings.

Temperature Guidelines:

Beef, Lamb, Veal (Medium-Rare): 130-135°F (54-57°C)
Pork (Medium): 145°F (63°C)
Chicken, Turkey: 165°F (74°C)
Fish: 145°F (63°C)

Tips for Consistent Results

Preheat Your Grill: Always preheat your grill for at least 10-15 minutes before cooking. This ensures that the grates are hot enough to sear the food properly.

Manage Flare-Ups: Flare-ups can cause uneven cooking and burnt food. Keep a spray bottle of water handy to control small flames.

Use a Timer: Timing is crucial, especially for foods that cook quickly. Use a timer to avoid overcooking.

Resting: Allow meats to rest for a few minutes after cooking. This helps the juices redistribute, resulting in more flavorful and tender meat.

Understanding heat and temperature is essential for becoming a proficient griller and smoker. By mastering these principles, you'll be able to cook a wide variety of foods to perfection, impressing your family and friends with every meal. Keep experimenting, stay patient, and enjoy the process of creating delicious, smoky, and perfectly grilled dishes. Happy grilling!

Preparing Your Ingredients

The success of any grilled or smoked dish starts with proper ingredient preparation. Selecting the right ingredients, marinating meats, prepping vegetables, and knowing the best methods for different foods can elevate your grilling and smoking game. This chapter will guide you through the essential steps to prepare your ingredients for a delicious and memorable meal.

Selecting Quality Ingredients

Choosing high-quality ingredients is the first step to great grilling and smoking. Here's what to look for:

Meats:

Beef: Look for marbling (the white streaks of fat within the muscle), which adds flavor and tenderness. Cuts like ribeye, sirloin, and brisket are excellent choices.
Pork: Select cuts with a good balance of meat and fat, such as pork shoulder, ribs, and chops. The fat helps keep the meat juicy during cooking.
Chicken: Opt for free-range or organic chicken for better flavor and texture. Whole chickens, thighs, and breasts are versatile choices.
Turkey: Turkey breasts and legs are ideal for grilling and smoking. Ensure the meat is fresh and has a pinkish color without any off smells.

Vegetables:

Freshness is key. Choose vegetables that are firm and free from blemishes. Popular grilling vegetables include bell peppers, zucchini, eggplant, mushrooms, and corn.

Seafood:

Look for bright, clear eyes and firm, shiny flesh. Fresh seafood should smell like the ocean, not fishy.
Salmon, shrimp, scallops, and tuna are excellent choices for grilling.

Marinating and Brining

Marinating and brining are techniques that enhance the flavor and texture of your food. Here's how to do it:

Purpose: Marinating adds flavor and helps tenderize the meat.
Ingredients: Common marinade ingredients include oil, acid (vinegar, lemon juice), herbs, spices, and aromatics (garlic, onions).

Time: Marinate meats for at least 30 minutes, but no longer than 24 hours. Seafood should marinate for a shorter period, typically 15-30 minutes.
Method: Place the meat in a resealable plastic bag or a covered dish and refrigerate. Turn occasionally to ensure even coverage.

Prepping Vegetables

Vegetables can be stars of the grill when prepared properly. Here's how to get them ready:

Cleaning: Wash all vegetables thoroughly to remove dirt and pesticides. Pat them dry with a paper towel.
Cutting: Cut vegetables into uniform pieces to ensure even cooking. For example, slice zucchini lengthwise, cut bell peppers into strips, and halve mushrooms.
Seasoning: Toss vegetables with olive oil, salt, and pepper. Add herbs and spices to enhance the flavor. Popular options include garlic powder, paprika, and rosemary.
Skewering: For smaller vegetables, use skewers to make handling easier. Soak wooden skewers in water for 30 minutes before using to prevent burning.

Prepping Meats

Properly prepping meats ensures they cook evenly and develop rich flavors. Here's how to do it:

Trimming: Remove excess fat and silver skin from meats to prevent flare-ups and ensure even cooking. Leave a thin layer of fat on cuts like steak and pork chops for added flavor.
Seasoning: Season meats generously with salt and pepper. Add dry rubs or spice blends for additional flavor. Let the seasoned meat sit at room temperature for 15-30 minutes before grilling.
Resting: After removing meats from the grill, let them rest for a few minutes. This allows the juices to redistribute, resulting in more tender and flavorful meat.

Preparing Seafood

Grilling seafood requires a delicate touch. Here's how to prepare it:

Cleaning: Rinse seafood under cold water and pat dry with a paper towel.
Seasoning: Season seafood lightly with salt, pepper, and a drizzle of olive oil. Add fresh herbs and citrus for a burst of flavor.
Skewering: Skewer shrimp, scallops, and smaller pieces of fish for easier handling and even cooking.
Handling: Use a fish basket or grill mat to prevent delicate fish from sticking to the grates and breaking apart.

Using Marinades, Rubs, and Sauces

Enhance your grilling and smoking with marinades, rubs, and sauces. Here's how to use them effectively:

Marinades:
Use marinades for meats and seafood to add flavor and tenderize. Make sure to discard used marinades or boil them if you plan to use them as a sauce.

Rubs:
Dry rubs are a blend of spices and herbs applied directly to the meat. They create a flavorful crust and can be used on meats, poultry, and vegetables.

Sauces:
Apply sauces during the last few minutes of grilling to prevent burning. Brush on barbecue sauce, teriyaki, or glaze to add a delicious finish.

Preparing your ingredients properly is a critical step in achieving great grilling and smoking results. By selecting quality ingredients, using marinades and brines, and prepping meats, vegetables, and seafood correctly, you set the foundation for delicious and memorable meals. With these tips and techniques, you'll be well on your way to grilling and smoking like a pro. Happy cooking!

Troubleshooting And Tips

Even the most experienced grill masters encounter challenges. From flare-ups to uneven cooking, various issues can arise that affect your grilling and smoking experience. This chapter will provide you with practical solutions to common problems and offer expert tips to ensure your grilling sessions are smooth and successful.

Common Grilling Problems and Solutions Flare-Ups

Problem: Fat drips onto the flames, causing flare-ups that can char the food.
Solution: Trim excess fat from meats and keep a spray bottle of water handy to douse small flames. Use a drip pan to catch fat and juices.

Uneven Cooking

Problem: Food cooks unevenly, with some parts overcooked and others undercooked.

Solution: Create heat zones on your grill (direct and indirect) to manage cooking temperatures better. Rotate food and move it between zones as needed.

Food Sticking to the Grates

Problem: Food sticks to the grill grates, making it difficult to turn and causing it to break apart.
Solution: Preheat the grill and oil the grates lightly before placing food on them. Use a spatula to gently lift food and prevent sticking.

Dry Meat

Problem: Meat becomes dry and tough after grilling.
Solution: Avoid overcooking by using a meat thermometer to check internal temperatures. Let meat rest after cooking to retain juices. Consider marinating or brining meats beforehand.

Burnt Exterior, Undercooked Interior

Problem: The outside of the food burns while the inside remains undercooked.
Solution: Use indirect heat for thicker cuts of meat and larger items. Sear the exterior on high heat, then move to a cooler zone to finish cooking.

Lack of Smoke Flavor

Problem: Smoked foods lack the desired smoky flavor.
Solution: Use the right type and amount of wood chips or chunks for your smoker. Soak wood chips in water for 30 minutes before adding to the smoker for a slower, more consistent burn.

Temperature Control Issues

Problem: Difficulty maintaining a consistent temperature on the grill or smoker.
Solution: Use a good-quality thermometer to monitor grill and smoker temperatures. Adjust vents on charcoal grills or burners on gas grills to regulate heat.

Expert Grilling Tips

Preheat the Grill
Always preheat your grill for at least 10-15 minutes before cooking. This ensures even heat distribution and helps prevent food from sticking.

Season the Grill Grates
Before placing food on the grill, lightly oil the grates using a paper towel soaked in oil and tongs. This creates a non-stick surface and adds flavor.

Use a Meat Thermometer
For perfectly cooked meats, invest in a reliable meat thermometer. Check the internal temperature to ensure doneness without overcooking.

Let Meat Rest
After grilling, allow meat to rest for a few minutes before slicing. This helps the juices redistribute, resulting in more flavorful and tender meat.

Marinate and Brine

Marinate meats for added flavor and tenderness. Brining helps keep meats juicy and enhances their natural flavors.

Keep a Clean Grill

Regularly clean your grill grates to prevent buildup and ensure optimal performance. A clean grill also reduces the risk of flare-ups and improves the taste of your food.

Master the Two-Zone Cooking Method
Create a direct heat zone for searing and an indirect heat zone for slower cooking. This method allows you to cook different types of food simultaneously and prevents burning.

Experiment with Wood Chips
For smokers, experiment with different types of wood chips (hickory, apple, mesquite) to find your preferred smoky flavor. Mix and match to create unique flavor profiles.

Use Aluminum Foil and Grill Baskets
Use aluminum foil to wrap delicate foods or create foil packets for easy grilling. Grill baskets are great for smaller items like vegetables and seafood, preventing them from falling through the grates.

Stay Organized
Keep all your grilling tools, seasonings, and ingredients within reach. Having everything organized and ready helps you focus on cooking and reduces stress.

Safety Tips

Location Matters
Place your grill on a stable, flat surface away from flammable materials and structures. Maintain a safe distance from the house, trees, and other potential hazards.

Monitor the Grill
Never leave your grill unattended while in use. Keep an eye on the flames and food to prevent accidents and overcooking.

Fire Safety

Have a fire extinguisher or a bucket of sand nearby in case of emergencies. Avoid using water on grease fires, as it can cause flare-ups.

Proper Lighting Techniques

Use chimney starters for charcoal grills instead of lighter fluid, which can leave a chemical taste. For gas grills, follow the manufacturer's instructions for safe ignition.

Handling Food Safely

Use separate cutting boards and utensils for raw and cooked foods to prevent cross-contamination. Wash your hands frequently, especially after handling raw meat.

Grilling and smoking are art forms that require practice and patience. By understanding common issues and employing expert tips, you can overcome challenges and enhance your grilling experience. Whether you're a novice or a seasoned pro, these troubleshooting techniques and tips will help you achieve delicious, perfectly cooked meals every time. Happy grilling

CHAPTER 2: 30-DAY MEAL PLAN

Day	Breakfast (600 kcal)	Lunch (600 kcal)	Snack (400 kcal)	Dinner (400 kcal)
Day 1	Grilled Breakfast Burrito with Eggs and Chorizo - p.21	Grilled Ribeye Steak with Garlic Butter and Rosemary Potatoes - p.35	Grilled Stuffed Jalapeños with Cream Cheese - p.50	Grilled Lemon Herb Chicken Breasts with Steamed Broccoli - p.57
Day 2	Grilled Breakfast Flatbread with Eggs and Bacon - p.22	Grilled Portobello Mushroom Burger with Swiss Cheese - p.33	Grilled Artichoke Hearts with Lemon Aioli - p.50	Grilled Pork Tenderloin Salad with Apples and Pecans - p.62
Day 3	Grilled Breakfast Quesadilla with Bacon and Cheese - p.23	Grilled Baby Back Ribs with BBQ Sauce and Coleslaw - p.38	Grilled Avocado Halves with Salsa - p.51	Grilled Salmon with Dill Yogurt Sauce - p.68
Day 4	Grilled Pancakes with Maple Syrup and Fresh Berries - p.30	Classic Grilled Cheeseburger - p.32	Smoky Grilled Eggplant Dip - p.52	Grilled Cauliflower Steaks with Romesco Sauce - p.65
Day 5	Grilled Cinnamon Rolls with Cream Cheese Icing - p.28	Grilled BBQ Chicken Thighs with Corn on the Cob - p.40	Grilled Artichoke Spinach Dip - p.52	Grilled Shrimp Skewers with Lemon Garlic Butter - p.68
Day 6	Grilled English Muffin - p.31	Grilled Pork Chops with Apple Glaze and Sautéed Spinach - p.45	Grilled Avocado and Mango Salsa - p.53	Grilled Tuna Steaks with Avocado Salsa - p.69
Day 7	Grilled Bacon and Egg Breakfast Sandwich - p.20	Grilled Spicy Turkey Sausage with Bell Peppers and Onions - p.42	Grilled Jalapeño and Lime Hummus - p.53	Grilled Halibut with Tomato Basil Relish - p.70
Day 8	Grilled Breakfast Skewers with Sausage and Veggies - p.28	Grilled Beef Tenderloin with Garlic and Herb Roasted Potatoes - p.48	Grilled Lemon Pound Cake with Berries - p.54	Grilled Vegetable Lasagna - p.72
Day 9	Grilled Breakfast Pizza with Eggs and Sausage - p.30	BBQ Bacon Cheeseburger - p.32	Grilled Blueberry Crisp - p.55	Grilled Chicken and Vegetable Skewers with Quinoa - p.58
Day 10	Grilled Mushroom and Spinach Frittata - p.21	Grilled Flank Steak with Soy-Ginger Marinade and Sesame Green Beans - p.35	Grilled Coconut Macaroons - p.55	Grilled Turkey Burgers with Spinach and Feta - p.57
Day 11	Grilled Breakfast Tacos with Chorizo and Eggs - p.23	Grilled Spare Ribs with Sweet and Spicy Glaze and Baked Beans - p.38	Grilled Pumpkin Pie Slices - p.56	Grilled Tilapia with Mango Salsa and Wild Rice - p.61
Day 12	Grilled Sausage and Hash Browns - p.20	Grilled Pork Tenderloin with Herb Rub and Roasted Sweet Potatoes - p.45	Grilled Cheesecake with Berry Compote - p.56	Grilled Eggplant Parmesan with Fresh Basil - p.59
Day 13	Grilled Chicken and Black Bean Quesadillas - p.24	Grilled Turkey Thighs with Garlic and Rosemary and Roasted Carrots - p.42	Grilled Pear and Blue Cheese Spread - p.54	Grilled BBQ Chicken Salad with Corn and Black Beans - p.64

Day	Breakfast (600 kcal)	Lunch (600 kcal)	Snack (400 kcal)	Dinner (400 kcal)
Day 14	Grilled Shrimp and Egg Tacos with Lime Crema - p.25	Grilled Sirloin Steak with Chimichurri Sauce and Grilled Asparagus - p.36	Grilled Halloumi Cheese with Lemon - p.51	Grilled Flank Steak and Arugula Salad - p.64
Day 15	Grilled Pork Sausage and Egg Tacos - p.25	Grilled Pork Sausages with Onions and German Potato Salad - p.47	Grilled Artichoke Spinach Dip - p.52	Grilled Swordfish with Pineapple Salsa - p.69
Day 16	Grilled Spicy Breakfast Tacos with Jalapeños - p.26	Grilled New York Strip with Balsamic Glaze and Roasted Brussels Sprouts - p.37	Grilled Avocado Halves with Salsa - p.51	Grilled Stuffed Tomatoes with Rice and Herbs - p.67
Day 17	Grilled Corn and Zucchini Quesadillas - p.27	Grilled Turkey Breast with Herb Marinade and Wild Rice Pilaf - p.43	Grilled Pumpkin Pie Slices - p.56	Grilled Ratatouille - p.65
Day 18	Grilled Lentil and Quinoa Breakfast Bowl - p.29	Grilled Beef and Veggie Stir-Fry with Jasmine Rice - p.49	Grilled Blueberry Crisp - p.55	Grilled Shrimp Skewers with Lemon Garlic Butter - p.68
Day 19	Grilled Bacon and Egg Salad - p.27	Grilled Pork Loin with Mustard Sauce and Green Bean Almondine - p.47	Grilled Jalapeño and Lime Hummus - p.53	Grilled Pork Tenderloin Salad with Apples and Pecans - p.62
Day 20	Grilled Greek Salad with Grilled Chicken and Feta - p.29	Grilled Ribeye Steak with Garlic Butter and Rosemary Potatoes - p.35	Grilled Lemon Pound Cake with Berries - p.54	Grilled Salmon with Dill Yogurt Sauce - p.68
Day 21	Grilled Breakfast Flatbread with Eggs and Bacon - p.22	Classic Grilled Cheeseburger - p.32	Grilled Avocado and Mango Salsa - p.53	Grilled Eggplant and Tomato Stack - p.61
Day 22	Grilled Breakfast Casserole with Sausage and Eggs - p.22	Grilled Pork Chops with Apple Glaze and Sautéed Spinach - p.45	Grilled Stuffed Jalapeños with Cream Cheese - p.50	Grilled BBQ Chicken Thighs with Corn on the Cob - p.40
Day 23	Grilled Breakfast Quesadilla with Bacon and Cheese - p.23	Grilled Turkey Meatballs with Spaghetti Squash - p.44	Grilled Halloumi Cheese with Lemon - p.51	Grilled Pork Sausages with Onions and German Potato Salad - p.47
Day 24	Grilled Breakfast Tacos with Chorizo and Eggs - p.23	Grilled Baby Back Ribs with BBQ Sauce and Coleslaw - p.38	Smoky Grilled Eggplant Dip - p.52	Grilled Tuna Steaks with Avocado Salsa - p.69
Day 25	Grilled Chicken and Black Bean Quesadillas - p.24	Grilled Portobello Mushroom Burger with Swiss Cheese - p.33	Grilled Artichoke Hearts with Lemon Aioli - p.50	Grilled Vegetable Wrap with Hummus - p.67
Day 26	Grilled Shrimp and Egg Tacos with Lime Crema - p.25	Grilled Flank Steak with Soy-Ginger Marinade and Sesame Green Beans - p.35	Grilled Coconut Macaroons - p.55	Grilled Chicken Caesar Salad with Light Dressing - p.60
Day 27	Grilled Pork Sausage and Egg Tacos - p.25	Grilled Sirloin Steak with Chimichurri Sauce and Grilled Asparagus - p.36	Grilled Artichoke Spinach Dip - p.52	Grilled Tilapia with Mango Salsa and Wild Rice - p.61
Day 28	Grilled Spicy Breakfast Tacos with Jalapeños - p.26	Grilled Turkey Thighs with Garlic and Rosemary and Roasted Carrots - p.42	Grilled Blueberry Crisp - p.55	Grilled Halloumi and Watermelon Salad - p.62

Day	Breakfast (600 kcal)	Lunch (600 kcal)	Snack (400 kcal)	Dinner (400 kcal)
Day 29	Grilled Corn and Zucchini Quesadillas - p.27	Grilled Beef Short Ribs with Red Wine Sauce and Garlic Mashed Potatoes - p.39	Grilled Jalapeño and Lime Hummus - p.53	Grilled Ratatouille - p.65
Day 30	Grilled Lentil and Quinoa Breakfast Bowl - p.29	BBQ Bacon Cheeseburger - p.32	Grilled Pear and Blue Cheese Spread - p.54	Grilled Swordfish with Pineapple Salsa - p.69

Note: The 30-Day Meal Plan provided in this book is intended as a guiding tool and a source of inspiration. The caloric values of the dishes can vary depending on portion sizes and specific ingredients used. Our meal plan is designed to offer a varied and balanced diet, rich in proteins, healthy fats, and carbohydrates, ensuring you can maintain healthy eating habits while enjoying delicious meals.

If you find that the calorie counts in the recipes do not align perfectly with your personal dietary needs or goals, feel free to adjust the portion sizes accordingly. Modify them up or down to tailor the meal plan to your unique requirements and preferences. Use your creativity and savor each meal in a way that best suits you!

CHAPTER 3: BREAKFASTS:
Classic Grilled Morning Feasts

Grilled Bacon and Egg Breakfast Sandwich

Prep: 10 minutes | Cook: 10 minutes | Serves: 2

Ingredients:

- 4 slices bacon (115g)
- 2 large eggs
- 2 slices cheddar cheese (60g)
- 2 English muffins, split (2 whole wheat rolls, 120g each)
- 1 tbsp butter (14g)
- Salt and pepper to taste

Instructions:

1. Preheat the grill to medium-high heat.
2. Grill the bacon until crispy, about 4-5 minutes per side. Remove and set aside.
3. Butter the English muffins and toast them on the grill until golden, about 1-2 minutes.
4. Grill the eggs on a flat griddle or skillet on the grill, seasoning with salt and pepper, until the whites are set, about 3-4 minutes.
5. Assemble the sandwich: place a slice of cheese, grilled egg, and bacon on the bottom half of each English muffin. Top with the other half of the muffin.

Nutritional Facts (Per Serving): Calories: 600 | Carbs: 36g | Protein: 26g | Fat: 40g | Fiber: 2g | Sodium: 1200mg | Sugars: 2g

Grilled Sausage and Hash Browns

Prep: 10 minutes | Cook: 20 minutes | Serves: 2

Ingredients:

- 4 sausage links (200g)
- 2 medium potatoes, shredded (300g)
- 2 tbsp olive oil (30ml)
- Salt and pepper to taste
- 1 small onion, diced (70g)

Instructions:

1. Preheat the grill to medium heat.
2. In a bowl, mix shredded potatoes, diced onion, olive oil, salt, and pepper.
3. Form the potato mixture into patties and place them on a greased grill pan or griddle.
4. Grill the patties for about 5-7 minutes per side, until crispy and golden brown.
5. Grill the sausages, turning occasionally, until fully cooked, about 10-12 minutes.Serve the grilled sausages with hash brown patties.

Nutritional Facts (Per Serving): Calories: 600 | Carbs: 40g | Protein: 20g | Fat: 40g | Fiber: 4g | Sodium: 1000mg | Sugars: 3g

Grilled Mushroom and Spinach Frittata

Prep: 10 minutes | Cook: 20 minutes | Serves: 2

Ingredients:

- 6 large eggs
- 1 cup fresh spinach, chopped (40g)
- 1 cup mushrooms, sliced (90g)
- 1/2 cup shredded mozzarella cheese (60g)
- 2 tbsp olive oil (30ml)
- Salt and pepper to taste

Instructions:

1. Preheat the grill to medium-high heat.
2. Heat 1 tbsp olive oil in a grill-safe skillet over medium heat. Sauté mushrooms until tender, about 5 minutes.
3. Add spinach to the skillet and cook until wilted, about 2 minutes.
4. In a bowl, whisk eggs, salt, and pepper. Pour over the vegetables in the skillet.
5. Sprinkle mozzarella cheese over the top.
6. Grill the frittata, with the lid closed, until the eggs are set and the cheese is melted, about 10-15 minutes.

Nutritional Facts (Per Serving): Calories: 600 | Carbs: 6g | Protein: 35g | Fat: 50g | Fiber: 2g | Sodium: 700mg | Sugars: 3g

Grilled Breakfast Burrito with Eggs and Chorizo

Prep: 10 minutes | Cook: 10 minutes | Serves: 2

Ingredients:

- 2 large eggs
- 1/2 cup cooked chorizo, crumbled (75g)
- 1/2 cup shredded cheddar cheese (50g)
- 2 large flour tortillas
- 1/4 cup diced tomatoes (40g)
- 1/4 cup diced onions (30g)
- 1 tbsp olive oil (15ml)
- 1/2 tsp salt

Instructions:

1. Preheat grill to medium heat.
2. In a pan, heat olive oil and sauté onions until translucent. Add tomatoes and cook for another 2 minutes.
3. Beat the eggs with salt and scramble them in the pan with the cooked vegetables.
4. Add chorizo to the eggs and mix well.
5. Place tortillas on the grill for 1-2 minutes until warm.
6. Fill each tortilla with the egg and chorizo mixture and top with shredded cheese.
7. Roll up the burritos and grill for another 2 minutes, turning occasionally, until lightly charred.

Nutritional Facts (Per Serving): Calories: 600 | Carbs: 42g | Protein: 30g | Fat: 32g | Fiber: 3g | Sodium: 1200mg | Sugars: 2g

Grilled Breakfast Flatbread with Eggs and Bacon

Prep: 15 minutes | Cook: 15 minutes | Serves: 2

Ingredients:

- 2 large eggs
- 2 pieces of flatbread
- 4 slices bacon, cooked and crumbled (50g)
- 1/2 cup shredded mozzarella cheese (50g)
- 1/4 cup diced bell peppers (40g)
- 1/4 cup sliced green onions (30g)
- 1 tbsp olive oil (15ml)
- 1/2 tsp salt

Instructions:

1. Preheat grill to medium-high heat.
2. Brush flatbreads with olive oil and place them on the grill for 2-3 minutes until slightly charred.
3. Beat the eggs with salt and scramble in a pan until just set.
4. Top each flatbread with scrambled eggs, bacon, bell peppers, green onions, and mozzarella cheese.
5. Place the flatbreads back on the grill, cover, and cook for 5 minutes until cheese is melted.

Nutritional Facts (Per Serving): Calories: 600 | Carbs: 40g | Protein: 34g | Fat: 30g | Fiber: 2g | Sodium: 1300mg | Sugars: 3g

Grilled Breakfast Casserole with Sausage and Eggs

Prep: 15 minutes | Cook: 30 minutes | Serves: 2

Ingredients:

- 6 large eggs
- 1/2 cup heavy cream (120ml)
- 1/2 lb breakfast sausage, crumbled and cooked (225g)
- 1 cup shredded cheddar cheese (100g)
- 1 cup diced bell peppers (150g)
- 1 cup diced onions (150g)
- 1 tsp salt
- 1 tbsp olive oil (15ml)

Instructions:

1. Preheat grill to medium heat.
2. In a skillet, heat olive oil and sauté onions and bell peppers until soft.
3. In a large bowl, whisk together eggs, heavy cream, and salt.
4. Stir in the cooked sausage, sautéed vegetables, and shredded cheese.
5. Pour the mixture into a greased cast iron skillet or grill-safe dish.
6. Place the skillet on the grill, cover, and cook for 25-30 minutes, until the eggs are set and the top is golden brown.

Nutritional Facts (Per Serving): Calories: 600 | Carbs: 8g | Protein: 36g | Fat: 48g | Fiber: 2g | Sodium: 1200mg | Sugars: 4g

CHAPTER 4: BREAKFAST: Flavorful Taco and Quesadilla Creations

Grilled Breakfast Quesadilla with Bacon and Cheese

Prep: 10 minutes | Cook: 10 minutes | Serves: 2

Ingredients:

- 4 slices bacon, cooked and crumbled (60g)
- 2 large flour tortillas
- 1 cup shredded cheddar cheese (100g)
- 1/4 cup diced tomatoes (40g)
- 1 tbsp olive oil (15ml)
- 1/2 tsp salt
- 2 large eggs

Instructions:

1. Preheat grill to medium heat.
2. In a pan, scramble the eggs with salt until just set.
3. Lay one tortilla on a flat surface and sprinkle half of the cheese, scrambled eggs, bacon, and tomatoes. Top with the other tortilla.
4. Brush the outside of the quesadilla with olive oil.
5. Grill the quesadilla for 3-4 minutes on each side until the cheese is melted and the tortilla is crispy.

Nutritional Facts (Per Serving): Calories: 600 | Carbs: 34g | Protein: 28g | Fat: 38g | Fiber: 2g | Sodium: 1100mg | Sugars: 3g

Grilled Breakfast Tacos with Chorizo and Eggs

Prep: 10 minutes | Cook: 15 minutes | Serves: 4

Ingredients:

- 8 oz chorizo sausage (225g)
- 8 large eggs
- 1/4 cup milk (60 ml)
- 1 cup shredded cheddar cheese (100g)
- 1/2 tsp salt
- 1/4 tsp black pepper
- 8 small flour tortillas
- 1 cup diced tomatoes (150g)
- 1/4 cup chopped cilantro (15g)

Instructions:

1. Preheat grill to medium-high heat.
2. Cook chorizo in a skillet over medium heat until browned, about 6 minutes.
3. Whisk together eggs, milk, salt, and pepper in a bowl. Pour over chorizo and cook, stirring until eggs are set, about 4 minutes.
4. Place tortillas on the grill for 1 minute per side, until warm and slightly charred.
5. Divide chorizo and egg mixture among tortillas. Top with cheese, tomatoes, and cilantro.

Nutritional Facts (Per Serving): Calories: 600 | Carbs: 25g | Protein: 29g | Fat: 41g | Fiber: 2g | Sodium: 900mg | Sugars: 3g

Grilled Chicken and Black Bean Quesadillas

Prep: 10 minutes | Cook: 10 minutes | Serves: 4

Ingredients:

- 8 small flour tortillas
- 1 cup shredded cooked turkey (150g)
- 1 1/2 cups shredded mozzarella cheese (150g)
- 1 ripe avocado, sliced
- 1/4 cup chopped cilantro (15g)
- 1/2 cup salsa (120 ml)
- 1/2 tsp salt
- 1/4 tsp black pepper

Instructions:

1. Preheat grill to medium-high heat.
2. Place 4 tortillas on a flat surface. Evenly distribute turkey, cheese, avocado slices, and cilantro on each tortilla. Sprinkle with salt and pepper.
3. Top with remaining tortillas to form quesadillas.
4. Grill quesadillas for 3-4 minutes per side, until cheese is melted and tortillas are crispy.

Nutritional Facts (Per Serving): Calories: 600 | Carbs: 32g | Protein: 31g | Fat: 36g | Fiber: 4g | Sodium: 750mg | Sugars: 3g

Grilled Chicken and Black Bean Quesadillas

Prep: 15 minutes | Cook: 10 minutes | Serves: 4

Ingredients:

- 2 cups shredded cooked chicken (300g)
- 1 cup canned black beans, drained and rinsed (250g)
- 1 1/2 cups shredded cheddar cheese (150g)
- 8 small flour tortillas
- 1/4 cup chopped cilantro (15g)
- 1/2 cup salsa (120 ml)
- 1/2 tsp ground cumin
- 1/2 tsp salt
- 1/4 tsp black pepper

Instructions:

1. Preheat grill to medium-high heat.
2. In a bowl, mix together chicken, black beans, cheese, cilantro, cumin, salt, and pepper.
3. Place 4 tortillas on a flat surface. Evenly distribute the chicken mixture on each tortilla.
4. Top with remaining tortillas to form quesadillas.
5. Grill quesadillas for 3-4 minutes per side, until cheese is melted and tortillas are crispy.

Nutritional Facts (Per Serving): Calories: 600 | Carbs: 34g | Protein: 39g | Fat: 28g | Fiber: 7g | Sodium: 800mg | Sugars: 2g

Grilled Shrimp and Egg Tacos with Lime Crema

Prep: 15 minutes | Cook: 10 minutes | Serves: 2

Ingredients:

- 12 large shrimp, peeled and deveined (200g)
- 4 large eggs
- 1 tbsp olive oil (15ml)
- 1 avocado, sliced (150g)
- 4 small corn tortillas (80g)
- 1/2 cup Greek yogurt (120g)
- Juice and zest of 1 lime
- 1/4 tsp salt
- 1/4 tsp black pepper
- Fresh cilantro for garnish

Instructions:

1. Preheat grill to medium-high heat. Toss shrimp with olive oil, salt, and pepper.

2. Grill shrimp for 2-3 minutes per side until pink and cooked through.

3. In a small bowl, whisk together Greek yogurt, lime juice, lime zest, and a pinch of salt to make the lime crema. Set aside.

4. In a nonstick skillet, scramble eggs over medium heat until just set.

5. Warm tortillas on the grill for about 30 seconds per side.

6. Assemble tacos by layering scrambled eggs, grilled shrimp, and avocado slices on each tortilla. Drizzle with lime crema and garnish with fresh cilantro.

Nutritional Facts (Per Serving): Calories: 600 | Sugars: 3g | Fat: 35g | Carbs: 30g | Protein: 35g | Fiber: 6g | Sodium: 800mg

Grilled Pork Sausage and Egg Tacos

Prep: 10 minutes | Cook: 15 minutes | Serves: 4

Ingredients:

- 1 lb pork sausage, sliced (450g)
- 8 large eggs
- 1/4 cup milk (60 ml)
- 1 cup shredded cheddar cheese (100g)
- 1/2 tsp salt
- 1/4 tsp black pepper
- 8 small flour tortillas
- 1/4 cup chopped cilantro (15g)
- 1/2 cup salsa (120 ml)
- 1 tbsp olive oil (15 ml)

Instructions:

1. Preheat grill to medium-high heat.

2 Cook sausage slices on the grill for 3-4 minutes per side, until fully cooked and browned. Set aside.

3. In a bowl, whisk together eggs, milk, salt, and pepper. Heat olive oil in a nonstick skillet over medium heat. Pour in the egg mixture and cook, stirring until scrambled and set, about 4 minutes.

4. Grill tortillas for 1 minute per side, until warm and slightly charred.

5. Divide scrambled eggs and grilled sausage among tortillas. Top with shredded cheese, cilantro, and salsa. Serve immediately.

Nutritional Facts (Per Serving): Calories: 600 | Carbs: 24g | Protein: 28g | Fat: 42g | Fiber: 1g | Sodium: 900mg | Sugars: 3g

Grilled Spicy Breakfast Tacos with Jalapeños

Prep: 10 minutes | Cook: 15 minutes | Serves: 4

Ingredients:

- 8 large eggs
- 1/4 cup milk (60 ml)
- 1 cup shredded pepper jack cheese (100g)
- 1/2 tsp salt
- 1/4 tsp black pepper
- 1 tbsp olive oil (15 ml)
- 1/2 cup diced onions (75g)
- 1/2 cup diced bell peppers (75g)
- 2 jalapeños, sliced
- 8 small flour tortillas
- 1/4 cup chopped cilantro (15g)
- 1/2 cup salsa (120 ml)

Instructions:

1. Preheat grill to medium-high heat.
2. In a bowl, whisk together eggs, milk, salt, and pepper.
3. Heat olive oil in a nonstick skillet over medium heat.
4. Add onions and bell peppers, sauté until softened, about 5 minutes.
5. Pour in the egg mixture and cook, stirring until scrambled and set, about 4 minutes.
6. Grill tortillas for 1 minute per side, until warm and slightly charred.

7. Divide scrambled eggs among tortillas. Top with cheese, jalapeños, cilantro, and salsa.

Nutritional Facts (Per Serving): Calories: 600 | Carbs: 26g | Protein: 28g | Fat: 39g | Fiber: 2g | Sodium: 850mg | Sugars: 3g

Grilled Mushroom and Spinach Quesadillas

Prep: 10 minutes | Cook: 15 minutes | Serves: 2

Ingredients:

- 4 large flour tortillas (4 large, 200g)
- 1 cup shredded mozzarella cheese (1 cup, 100g)
- 1 cup mushrooms, sliced (1 cup, 90g)
- 2 tbsp olive oil (2 tbsp, 30ml)
- 1/2 tsp salt (1/2 tsp, 3g)
- 1/2 tsp black pepper (1/2 tsp, 1g)
- 1 cup fresh spinach, chopped (1 cup, 40g)

Instructions:

1. Preheat grill to medium heat.
2. In a pan, heat 1 tbsp (15ml) olive oil over medium heat. Sauté mushrooms until tender.
3. Add spinach and cook until wilted. Season with salt and pepper. Set aside.
4. Brush one side of each tortilla with the remaining olive oil. Place tortillas, oiled side down, on a clean surface.
5. Sprinkle half of the cheese on one half of each tortilla. Top with the mushroom and spinach

mixture, then sprinkle the remaining cheese.
6. Fold tortillas in half and place on the grill. Cook for 2-3 minutes per side until the tortillas are golden and the cheese is melted.

Nutritional Facts (Per Serving): Calories: 600 | Carbs: 45g | Protein: 20g | Fat: 35g | Fiber: 4g | Sodium: 800mg | Sugars: 4g

Grilled Corn and Zucchini Quesadillas

Prep: 10 minutes | Cook: 15 minutes | Serves: 2

Ingredients:

- 4 large flour tortillas (4 large, 200g)
- 1 cup shredded cheddar cheese (1 cup, 100g)
- 1 cup grilled corn kernels (1 cup, 160g)
- 2 tbsp olive oil (2 tbsp, 30ml)
- 1/2 tsp salt (1/2 tsp, 3g)
- 1/2 tsp black pepper (1/2 tsp, 1g)
- 1 cup zucchini, thinly sliced (1 cup, 130g)

Instructions:

1. Arrange the sliced cucumber around the edges of each plate.
2. Place a generous scoop of cottage cheese in the center of each plate.
3. Sprinkle the chopped walnuts over the cottage cheese.
4. Drizzle olive oil over the cottage cheese and

cucumbers, then sprinkle with fresh ground black pepper.

Nutritional Facts (Per Serving): Calories: 750 | Carbs: 9g | Protein: 40g | Fat: 62g | Fiber: 2g | Sodium: 900mg | Sugars: 5g

Bacon and Egg Salad

Prep: 10 minutes| Cook: 10 mins | Serves: 2

Ingredients:

- large eggs, hard-boiled and chopped
- 12 slices bacon, cooked crisp and crumbled
- 1/2 cup full-fat Greek yogurt (120ml)
- 2 tbsp Dijon mustard (30ml)
- Salt and pepper to taste
- Optional: 4 tbsp chopped chives for garnish

Instructions:

1. Cook bacon until crisp and boil eggs. Once cooked, chop eggs and crumble bacon.
2. In a large bowl, mix chopped eggs, crumbled bacon, Greek yogurt, and Dijon mustard. Season with salt and pepper.
3. Garnish with chives if using, and serve chilled or at room temperature.

Nutritional Facts (Per Serving): Calories: 750 | Carbs: 9g | Protein: 40g | Fat: 62g | Fiber: 0g | Sodium: 1300mg | Sugars: 1g

CHAPTER 5: BREAKFASTS: Energizing Protein-Powered Breakfasts

Grilled Breakfast Skewers with Sausage and Veggies

Prep: 10 minutes | Cook: 15 minutes | Serves: 2

Ingredients:

- 8 oz breakfast sausage links, cut into chunks (225g)
- 1 cup cherry tomatoes (150g)
- 1 cup bell peppers, cut into chunks (150g)
- 1 small red onion, cut into chunks (70g)
- 2 tbsp olive oil (30 ml)
- 1 tsp dried oregano (2g)
- 1/2 tsp salt
- 1/2 tsp black pepper

Instructions:

1. Preheat grill to medium-high heat.
2. In a large bowl, toss sausage chunks, cherry tomatoes, bell peppers, and red onion with olive oil, oregano, salt, and black pepper.
3. Thread sausage and vegetables onto skewers.
4. Grill skewers for 10-15 minutes, turning occasionally, until sausages are cooked through and vegetables are tender.

Nutritional Facts (Per Serving): Calories: 600 | Carbs: 10g | Protein: 20g | Fat: 50g | Fiber: 3g | Sodium: 800mg | Sugars: 5g

Grilled Cinnamon Rolls with Cream Cheese Icing

Prep: 15 minutes | Cook: 20 minutes | Serves: 2

Ingredients:

- 4 premade cinnamon rolls (400g)
- 4 oz cream cheese, softened (115g)
- 1/4 cup unsalted butter, softened (60g)
- 1 cup powdered low carb sweetener (100g)
- 1/2 tsp vanilla extract (2.5 ml)
- 1 tbsp heavy cream (15 ml)

Instructions:

1. Preheat the grill to medium heat.
2. Place cinnamon rolls on the grill, cut side down. Grill for 3-5 minutes until they have grill marks and are heated through.
3. In a bowl, beat together cream cheese, butter, powdered low carb sweetener, vanilla extract, and heavy cream until smooth and creamy.
4. Spread the cream cheese icing over the grilled cinnamon rolls.

Nutritional Facts (Per Serving): Calories: 600 | Carbs: 36g | Protein: 6g | Fat: 50g | Fiber: 2g | Sodium: 400mg | Sugars: 6g

Grilled Greek Salad with Grilled Chicken and Feta

Prep: 15 minutes | Cook: 15 minutes | Serves: 2

Ingredients:

- 2 boneless, skinless chicken breasts (300g)
- 2 tbsp olive oil (30ml)
- 1 tsp dried oregano
- 1/2 tsp salt
- 1/4 tsp black pepper
- 1 head romaine lettuce, chopped (300g)
- 1 cup cherry tomatoes, halved (150g)
- 1/2 cucumber, sliced (100g)
- 1/4 red onion, thinly sliced (50g)
- 1/2 cup Kalamata olives (75g)
- 1/2 cup crumbled feta cheese (75g)
- 1 tbsp lemon juice (15ml)

Instructions:

1. Preheat the grill to medium-high heat.
2. Rub the chicken breasts with 1 tbsp olive oil, oregano, salt, and pepper.
3. Grill the chicken for 6-7 minutes per side, or until fully cooked. Let rest for 5 minutes, then slice.
4. In a large bowl, combine the chopped romaine, cherry tomatoes, cucumber, red onion, and olives.
5. Top the salad with sliced grilled chicken and crumbled feta cheese.
6. Drizzle with remaining olive oil and lemon juice.

Nutritional Facts (Per Serving): Calories: 600 | Carbs: 20g | Protein: 40g | Fat: 40g | Fiber: 8g | Sodium: 1000mg | Sugars: 8g

Grilled Lentil and Quinoa Breakfast Bowl

Prep: 15 minutes | Cook: 20 minutes | Serves: 2

Ingredients:

- 1/2 cup quinoa (85g)
- 1/2 cup cooked lentils (100g)
- 1 tbsp olive oil (15 ml)
- 1 red bell pepper, diced (150g)
- 1 zucchini, sliced (200g)
- 1/2 red onion, sliced (75g)
- 1 cup cherry tomatoes, halved (150g)
- 1/2 cup feta cheese, crumbled (75g)
- 1 tbsp lemon juice (15 ml)
- 1 tsp dried oregano (5g)
- 1/2 tsp salt (2.5g)
- 1/2 tsp black pepper (2.5g)
- 2 large eggs

Instructions:

1. Preheat grill to medium-high heat.
Cook quinoa as per package instructions and set aside.
Toss red bell pepper, zucchini, red onion, and cherry tomatoes with olive oil, oregano, salt, and pepper. Grill for 10-15 minutes until tender.
Mix cooked quinoa, lentils, grilled vegetables, feta cheese, and lemon juice in a bowl.
Grill eggs to desired doneness.
Divide quinoa mixture into bowls and top with grilled eggs.

Nutritional Facts (Per Serving): Calories: 600 | Carbs: 55g | Protein: 26g | Fat: 30g | Fiber: 12g | Sodium: 800mg | Sugars: 8g

CHAPTER 6: BREAKFAST: Indulgent Weekend Brunch Inspirations

Grilled Breakfast Pizza with Eggs and Sausage

Prep: 10 minutes | Cook: 15 minutes | Serves: 2

Ingredients:

- 1 pre-made pizza crust (200g)
- 1/2 cup pizza sauce (120ml)
- 1 cup shredded mozzarella cheese (100g))
- 2 large eggs
- 2 breakfast sausages, cooked and crumbled (100g)
- 1/4 cup chopped green onions (25g)
- 1/2 tsp dried oregano (2.5g)
- 1 tbsp olive oil (15ml)

Instructions:

1.Preheat grill to medium-high heat.
2. Spread pizza sauce on crust, then add mozzarella cheese. Create two wells in the cheese and crack an egg into each.
4. Top with crumbled sausage, chopped green onions, oregano, and a drizzle of olive oil.
5. Grill with the lid closed for 10-15 minutes until eggs are set and crust is crispy.
Nutritional Facts (Per Serving): Calories: 600 | Carbs: 45g | Protein: 30g | Fat: 35g | Fiber: 2g | Sodium: 1000mg | Sugars: 5g

Grilled Pancakes with Maple Syrup and Fresh Berries

Prep: 10 minutes | Cook: 10 minutes | Serves: 2

Ingredients:

- 1 cup pancake mix (120g)
- 3/4 cup water (180ml)
- 1/2 tsp vanilla extract (2.5ml)
- 1 tbsp butter, melted (15g)
- 1/2 cup maple syrup (120ml)
- 1 cup mixed fresh berries (150g)
- 1/4 cup low carb sweetener (50g)

Instructions:

1. Preheat the grill to medium heat and lightly oil the griddle.
2. In a bowl, mix pancake mix, water, vanilla extract, and melted butter until smooth.
3. Pour 1/4 cup (60ml) of the batter onto the griddle for each pancake.
4. Grill the pancakes until bubbles form on the surface and the edges look dry, then flip and cook until golden brown, about 2-3 minutes per side.
5. Serve the pancakes with maple syrup and fresh berries, and sprinkle with low carb sweetener.

Nutritional Facts (Per Serving): Calories: 600 | Carbs: 80g | Protein: 8g | Fat: 18g | Fiber: 4g | Sodium: 500mg | Sugars: 35g

Grilled English Muffin

Prep: 10 minutes | Cook: 10 minutes | Serves: 2

Ingredients:

- 2 English muffins, split and toasted
- 4 large eggs
- 1/4 cup heavy cream (60 ml)
- 1 tbsp butter (14g)
- 4 oz smoked salmon (115g)
- 1 tbsp chopped chives (10g)
- Salt and pepper to taste

Instructions:

1. Preheat grill to medium-high.
2. Whisk eggs, heavy cream, salt, and pepper in a bowl.
3. Melt butter in a pan over medium heat, add egg mixture, and scramble until just set.
4. Grill English muffins until golden brown.
5. Top muffins with scrambled eggs, smoked salmon, and chopped chives.

Nutritional Facts (Per Serving): Calories: 600 | Carbs: 30g | Protein: 28g | Fat: 38g | Fiber: 2g | Sodium: 1200mg | Sugars: 3g

Casserole with grilled vegetables and feta for breakfast

Prep: 15 minutes | Cook: 30 minutes | Serves: 2

Ingredients:

- 1 cup bell peppers, sliced (150g)
- 1 cup zucchini, sliced (130g)
- 1 cup cherry tomatoes, halved (160g)
- 1 small red onion, sliced (70g))
- 2 tbsp olive oil (30ml)
- 6 large eggs
- 1/2 cup heavy cream (120ml)
- 1 cup crumbled feta cheese (150g)
- 1 tsp dried oregano
- Salt and pepper to taste

Instructions:

1. Preheat the grill to medium-high heat.
2. Toss the bell peppers, zucchini, cherry tomatoes, and red onion with olive oil, salt, and pepper. Grill the vegetables until they are tender and slightly charred, about 10 minutes.
3. Preheat the oven to 375°F (190°C). In a large bowl, whisk together the eggs, heavy cream, oregano, salt, and pepper. Stir in the grilled vegetables and crumbled feta cheese.
4. Pour the mixture into a greased baking dish. Bake for 25 minutes, or until the casserole is set and golden on top.

Nutritional Facts (Per Serving): Calories: 600 | Carbs: 15g | Protein: 25g | Fat: 48g | Fiber: 4g | Sodium: 1000mg | Sugars: 10g

CHAPTER 7: LUNCHES: Delectable Burger and Sandwich Delights

Classic Grilled Cheeseburger

Prep: 10 minutes | Cook: 20 minutes | Serves: 2

Ingredients:

- 1 lb ground beef (450g)
- 2 hamburger buns
- 4 slices cheddar cheese
- 1 large onion, thinly sliced (150g)
- 2 tbsp butter (30g)
- Salt and pepper to taste
- 2 tbsp low carb sweeteners (30g)

Instructions:

1. Form ground beef into 2 patties, season with salt and pepper.
2. Grill patties over medium heat for 4-5 minutes per side, adding cheese in the last minute.
3. In a skillet, melt butter over medium heat, caramelize onions for 10-15 minutes, then add low carb sweetener and cook for 2 more minutes.
4. Toast hamburger buns on the grill for 1-2 minutes. Assemble burgers with patties, caramelized onions, and desired toppings.

Nutritional Facts (Per Serving): Calories: 600 | Sugars: 6g | Fat: 38g | Carbs: 30g | Protein: 32g | Fiber: 2g | Sodium: 800mg

BBQ Bacon Cheeseburger

Prep: 15 minutes | Cook: 20 minutes | Serves: 2

Ingredients:

- 8 oz ground beef (225g)
- 4 slices bacon (100g)
- 2 hamburger buns (150g)
- 4 slices cheddar cheese (100g)
- 1 cup crispy fried onions (80g)
- 2 tbsp BBQ sauce (30ml)
- Salt and pepper to taste
- 2 lettuce leaves
- 2 tomato slices

Instructions:

1. Preheat grill to medium-high heat.
2. Form ground beef into 2 patties, season with salt and pepper.
3. Grill patties for 4-5 minutes per side. Add cheddar cheese slices in the last minute to melt.
4. Cook bacon on the grill or in a pan until crispy.
5. Toast hamburger buns on the grill for 1-2 minutes. Assemble burgers with BBQ sauce, lettuce, tomato, cheese-topped patties, bacon, and fried onions.

Nutritional Facts (Per Serving): Calories: 600 | Sugars: 7g | Fat: 35g | Carbs: 40g | Protein: 35g | Fiber: 3g | Sodium: 1200mg

Grilled Portobello Mushroom Burger with Swiss Cheese

Prep: 10 minutes | Cook: 20 minutes | Serves: 2

Ingredients:

- 2 large portobello mushrooms (200g each)
- 2 Tbsp olive oil (30ml)
- 2 tsp balsamic vinegar (10ml)
- 2 slices Swiss cheese (60g total)
- 2 whole-grain burger buns (120g total)
- 1 cup arugula (30g)
- 1 medium tomato, sliced (150g)
- Salt and pepper to taste

Instructions:

1. Preheat the grill to medium heat.
2. Brush portobello mushrooms with olive oil and balsamic vinegar. Season with salt and pepper.
3. Grill mushrooms gill-side up for 5 minutes. Flip and grill for another 3 minutes.
4. Place a slice of Swiss cheese on each mushroom and grill until melted, about 2 minutes.
5. Toast burger buns on the grill for 1-2 minutes until golden.
6. Assemble the burgers with grilled mushrooms, arugula, and tomato slices.

Nutritional Facts (Per Serving): Calories: 600 | Sugars: 6g | Fat: 32g | Carbs: 56g | Protein: 24g | Fiber: 8g | Sodium: 1000mg

Spicy Jalapeño Burger with Pepper Jack Cheese

Prep: 15 minutes | Cook: 15 minutes | Serves: 2

Ingredients:

- 1 lb ground beef (450g)
- 2 jalapeños, diced (30g)
- 2 slices pepper jack cheese (50g)
- 2 whole wheat burger buns (100g)
- 1 avocado, sliced (150g)
- 2 tbsp Greek yogurt (30ml)
- 1 tomato, sliced (120g)
- 1/2 cup lettuce leaves (25g)
- Salt and pepper to taste

Instructions:

1. Preheat grill to medium-high heat. Mix ground beef with diced jalapeños, salt, and pepper. Form into 2 patties.
2. Grill patties for 5-6 minutes per side, or until desired doneness. Place a slice of pepper jack cheese on each patty during the last minute of cooking.
3. Toast the burger buns on the grill until golden brown.
4. Spread 1 tbsp Greek yogurt on each bun half.
5. Assemble the burgers with grilled patties, avocado slices, tomato slices, and lettuce.

Nutritional Facts (Per Serving): Calories: 600 | Sugars: 4g | Fat: 35g | Carbs: 30g | Protein: 35g | Fiber: 8g | Sodium: 800mg

Grilled Chicken Club Sandwich with Avocado

Prep: 15 minutes | Cook: 20 minutes | Serves: 2

Ingredients:

- 2 chicken breasts (300g each)
- 4 slices of whole wheat bread (100g)
- 4 slices of cooked bacon (80g)
- 1 avocado, sliced (150g)
- 2 tbsp Greek yogurt (30ml)
- 1 tomato, sliced (120g)
- 1 cup lettuce leaves (50g)
- Salt and pepper to taste

Instructions:

1. Season chicken breasts with salt and pepper. Grill over medium heat until fully cooked, about 6-7 minutes per side.
2. Toast the whole wheat bread slices until golden brown.
3. Spread 1 tbsp Greek yogurt on each slice of bread.
4. Layer grilled chicken, bacon, avocado slices, tomato, and lettuce between the bread slices.
5. Cut each sandwich in half and serve immediately.

Nutritional Facts (Per Serving): Calories: 600 | Sugars: 6g | Fat: 28g | Carbs: 35g | Protein: 45g | Fiber: 10g | Sodium: 900mg

Turkey Burger with Cranberry Sauce

Prep: 15 minutes| Cook: 45 mins | Serves: 4

Ingredients:

- 1 lb ground turkey (450g)
- 1/4 cup breadcrumbs (30g)
- 1 egg, beaten
- 2 tbsp chopped fresh parsley (8g)
- 1/2 tsp salt (3g)
- 1/4 tsp black pepper (1g)
- 2 whole wheat burger buns (100g)
- 1/4 cup cranberry sauce (60g)
- 1/2 cup lettuce leaves (25g)
- 1 tomato, sliced (120g)

Instructions:

1. Preheat grill to medium-high heat. In a bowl, mix ground turkey, breadcrumbs, egg, parsley, salt, and pepper. Form into 2 patties.
2. Grill patties for 5-6 minutes per side, or until fully cooked.
3. Toast the burger buns on the grill until golden brown.
4. Spread cranberry sauce on the top half of each bun.
5. Assemble the burgers with grilled patties, lettuce, and tomato slices.

Nutritional Facts (Per Serving): Calories: 600 | Sugars: 8g | Fat: 22g | Carbs: 45g | Protein: 35g | Fiber: 6g | Sodium: 700mg

Grilled Ribeye Steak with Garlic Butter and Rosemary Potatoes

Prep: 15 minutes | Cook: 20 minutes | Serves: 2

Ingredients:

- 2 ribeye steaks (300g each)
- 2 tbsp unsalted butter (30g)
- 3 cloves garlic, minced (9g)
- 1 tbsp fresh rosemary, chopped (15g)
- 2 medium potatoes, cubed (400g)
- 2 tbsp olive oil (30ml)
- Salt and pepper to taste

Instructions:

1. Preheat grill to medium-high heat.
2. Rub ribeye steaks with salt and pepper.
3. Mix butter, garlic, and rosemary in a small bowl.
4. Toss cubed potatoes with olive oil, salt, and pepper.
5. Grill potatoes for about 15 minutes, turning occasionally.
6. Grill steaks for 4-5 minutes per side for medium-rare.
7. Top steaks with garlic butter and let rest.
8. Serve steaks with grilled rosemary potatoes.

Nutritional Facts (Per Serving): Calories: 600 | Sugars: 1g | Fat: 38g | Carbs: 30g | Protein: 40g | Fiber: 4g | Sodium: 400mg

Grilled Flank Steak with Soy-Ginger Marinade and Sesame Green Beans

Prep: 20 minutes | Cook: 15 minutes | Serves: 2

Ingredients:

- 1 lb flank steak (450g)
- 1/4 cup soy sauce (60ml)
- 2 tbsp olive oil (30ml)
- 2 tbsp low carb sweeteners (25g)
- 2 tbsp fresh ginger, grated (25g)
- 2 cloves garlic, minced (10g)
- 1 tsp sesame oil (5ml)
- 1 lb green beans, trimmed (450g)
- 1 tbsp sesame seeds (15g)
- Salt and pepper to taste

Instructions:

1. In a bowl, mix soy sauce, olive oil, low carb sweeteners, grated ginger, and minced garlic. Marinate flank steak in this mixture for 15 minutes.
2. Preheat the grill to medium-high heat. Grill flank steak for 5-6 minutes per side, or until desired doneness. Remove from grill and let rest.
3. While steak rests, toss green beans with sesame oil, salt, and pepper. Grill for 5 minutes until tender.
4. Slice flank steak against the grain and serve with sesame green beans, topped with sesame seeds.

Nutritional Facts (Per Serving): Calories: 600 | Sugars: 2g | Fat: 30g | Carbs: 10g | Protein: 55g | Fiber: 5g | Sodium: 900mg

Grilled Sirloin Steak with Chimichurri Sauce and Grilled Asparagus

Prep: 15 minutes | Cook: 20 minutes | Serves: 2

Ingredients:

- 2 sirloin steaks (8 oz each) (227g each)
- 1 bunch asparagus, trimmed (300g)
- 2 tbsp olive oil (30ml)
- Salt and pepper to taste
- 1 cup fresh parsley, chopped (60g)
- 1/2 cup fresh cilantro, chopped (30g)
- 4 cloves garlic, minced (12g)
- 1/4 cup red wine vinegar (60ml)
- 1/2 cup olive oil (120ml)
- 1 tsp red pepper flakes (5g)

Instructions:

1. Combine parsley, cilantro, garlic, red wine vinegar, 1/2 cup olive oil, and red pepper flakes in a bowl. Mix well and set aside.
2. Rub steaks with 2 tbsp olive oil, salt, and pepper.
3. Preheat grill to high heat. Grill steaks for 4-5 minutes per side for medium-rare. Let rest for 5 minutes.
4. Toss asparagus with olive oil, salt, and pepper. Grill for 5-7 minutes until tender.
5. Slice steaks, drizzle with chimichurri sauce, and serve with grilled asparagus.

Nutritional Facts (Per Serving): Calories: 600 | Sugars: 2g | Fat: 45g | Carbs: 8g | Protein: 40g | Fiber: 4g | Sodium: 400mg

Grilled T-Bone Steak with Herb Butter and Creamed Spinach

Prep: 15 minutes | Cook: 20 minutes | Serves: 2

Ingredients:

- 2 T-Bone steaks (350g each)
- 4 tbsp unsalted butter (60g)
- 1 tbsp chopped fresh parsley (15g)
- 1 tsp chopped fresh thyme (5g)
- 1 tsp chopped fresh rosemary (5g)
- Salt and pepper to taste
- 10 oz fresh spinach (300g)
- 1/2 cup heavy cream (120ml)
- 2 tbsp grated Parmesan cheese (30g)
- 1 clove garlic, minced (5g)

Instructions:

1. Preheat grill to medium-high heat.
2. Season T-Bone steaks with salt and pepper.
3. Grill steaks for 5-7 minutes per side for medium-rare.
4. Mix softened butter with parsley, thyme, rosemary, and salt.
5. Sauté garlic in butter, add spinach and cook until wilted.
6. Stir in heavy cream and Parmesan, cook until thickened.
7. Serve steaks with herb butter and creamed spinach.

Nutritional Facts (Per Serving): Calories: 600 | Sugars: 2g | Fat: 45g | Carbs: 5g | Protein: 45g | Fiber: 2g | Sodium: 500mg

Grilled Filet Mignon with Blue Cheese Butter and Mashed Cauliflower

Prep: 20 minutes | Cook: 30 minutes | Serves: 2

Ingredients:

- 2 (6 oz) filet mignon steaks (170g each)
- 2 tbsp olive oil (30ml)
- Salt and pepper to taste
- 2 tbsp butter (30g)
- 2 oz blue cheese, crumbled (55g)
- 1 head cauliflower, chopped (500g)
- 1/4 cup heavy cream (60ml)
- 2 cloves garlic, minced (2 cloves, 10g)

Instructions:

1. Preheat grlll to medium-high heat. Rub steaks with olive oil, salt, and pepper.
2. Grill steaks for 4-5 minutes per side for medium-rare. Adjust timing based on desired doneness.
3. In a small bowl, mix butter and blue cheese. Set aside.
4. Steam cauliflower until tender, about 10 minutes.
5. Drain and mash with heavy cream and garlic until smooth. Season with salt and pepper.
6. Top each steak with blue cheese butter. Serve with mashed cauliflower.

Nutritional Facts (Per Serving): Calories: 600 | Sugars: 4g | Fat: 42g | Carbs: 10g | Protein: 40g | Fiber: 4g | Sodium: 400mg

Grilled New York Strip with Balsamic Glaze and Roasted Brussels Sprouts

Prep: 15 minutes | Cook: 25 minutes | Serves: 2

Ingredients:

- 2 New York strip steaks (8 oz each) (225g each)
- 1 tbsp olive oil (15 ml)
- Salt and pepper to taste
- 1/4 cup balsamic vinegar (60 ml)
- 1 tbsp low carb sweetener (15g)
- 1 lb Brussels sprouts, halved (450g)
- 2 tbsp olive oil (30 ml)
- Salt and pepper to taste

Instructions:

1. Preheat grill to medium-high heat. Rub steaks with 1 tbsp olive oil, salt, and pepper.
2. Grill steaks for 4-5 minutes per side for medium-rare, or until desired doneness. Let rest.
3. In a small saucepan, bring balsamic vinegar and low carb sweetener to a boil. Reduce heat and simmer until thickened, about 5 minutes.
4. Toss Brussels sprouts with 2 tbsp olive oil, salt, and pepper. Roast in preheated oven at 400°F (200°C) for 20 minutes, until tender and caramelized.
5. Serve steaks drizzled with balsamic glaze alongside roasted Brussels sprouts.

Nutritional Facts (Per Serving): Calories: 600 | Sugars: 6g | Fat: 40g | Carbs: 20g | Protein: 45g | Fiber: 6g | Sodium: 800m

Grilled Baby Back Ribs with BBQ Sauce and Coleslaw

Prep: 20 minutes | Cook: 2 hours | Serves: 2

Ingredients:

- 1 rack baby back ribs (1.5 lbs) (700g)
- 1/4 cup BBQ sauce (60ml)
- 1/4 cup low-carb sweetener (50g)
- 1/2 head cabbage, shredded (300g)
- 1 carrot, shredded (50g)
- 1/4 cup Greek yogurt (60ml)
- 1 tbsp apple cider vinegar (15ml)
- Salt and pepper to taste

Instructions:

1. Preheat grill to medium heat. Season ribs with salt and pepper.
2. Grill ribs over indirect heat for 1.5 to 2 hours, basting with BBQ sauce in the last 30 minutes.
3. In a bowl, mix shredded cabbage, carrot, greek yogurt, apple cider vinegar, salt, and pepper to make coleslaw.
4. Serve ribs with a side of coleslaw.

Nutritional Facts (Per Serving): Calories: 600 | Sugars: 12g | Fat: 40g | Carbs: 20g | Protein: 40g | Fiber: 5g | Sodium: 1200mg

Grilled Spare Ribs with Sweet and Spicy Glaze and Baked Beans

Prep: 20 minutes | Cook: 2 hours | Serves: 2

Ingredients:

- 1 rack spare ribs (2 lbs) (900g)
- 1/2 cup BBQ sauce (120ml)
- 2 tbsp honey (30ml)
- 1 tbsp hot sauce (15ml)
- 1 tbsp olive oil (15ml)
- 1 can baked beans (15 oz) (425g)
- 1/4 cup diced onions (30g)
- 1 tsp low carb sweeteners (5g)
- Salt and pepper to taste

Instructions:

1. Preheat grill to medium heat.
2. Mix BBQ sauce, honey, hot sauce, and low carb sweeteners in a bowl for the glaze.
3. Rub ribs with olive oil, salt, and pepper.
4. Grill ribs for 1.5 to 2 hours, basting with the glaze every 20 minutes.
5. Heat baked beans in a saucepan with diced onions until warm.
6. Serve ribs with baked beans on the side.

Nutritional Facts (Per Serving): Calories: 600 | Sugars: 15g | Fat: 25g | Carbs: 45g | Protein: 30g | Fiber: 6g | Sodium: 1400mg

Grilled Country Style Ribs with Mustard Sauce and Potato Salad

Prep: 20 minutes | Cook: 1 hour 30 minutes | Serves: 2

Ingredients:

- 1 lb country style ribs (450g)
- 1/4 cup yellow mustard (60ml)
- 2 tbsp low-carb sweetener (30g)
- 1 lb potatoes, diced (450g)
- 1/4 cup Greek yogurt (60ml)
- 1 tbsp Dijon mustard (15ml)
- 1 tbsp apple cider vinegar (15ml)
- 2 tbsp chopped dill (8g)
- Salt and pepper to taste

Instructions:

1. Preheat grill to medium heat. Season ribs with salt and pepper.

2. Grill ribs over indirect heat for 1 to 1.5 hours, basting with yellow mustard mixed with low-carb sweetener in the last 30 minutes.

3. Boil diced potatoes until tender, about 10 minutes. Drain and let cool.

4. In a bowl, mix Greek yogurt, Dijon mustard, apple cider vinegar, dill, salt, and pepper. Add cooled potatoes and mix well to make potato salad.

5. Serve ribs with a side of potato salad.

Nutritional Facts (Per Serving): Calories: 600 | Sugars: 8g | Fat: 30g | Carbs: 45g | Protein: 30g | Fiber: 5g | Sodium: 800mg.

Grilled Beef Short Ribs with Red Wine Sauce and Garlic Mashed Potatoes

Prep: 20 minutes | Cook: 1 hour 30 minutes | Serves: 2

Ingredients:

- 1.5 lbs beef short ribs (680g)
- 2 tbsp olive oil (30ml)
- 1 cup red wine (240ml)
- 1 cup beef broth (240ml)
- 2 garlic cloves, minced (10g)
- Salt and pepper to taste
- 2 large potatoes, peeled and diced (400g)
- 1/4 cup heavy cream (60ml)
- 2 tbsp butter (30g)
- 1 tsp low carb sweeteners (5g)

Instructions:

1. Preheat grill to medium heat.

2. Rub short ribs with olive oil, salt, and pepper.

3. Grill short ribs for 1.5 hours, turning occasionally.

4. In a saucepan, combine red wine, beef broth, minced garlic, and low carb sweeteners. Simmer until reduced by half.

5. For mashed potatoes, boil potatoes until tender, then mash with heavy cream, butter, minced garlic, salt, and pepper.

6. Serve short ribs with red wine sauce drizzled over and garlic mashed potatoes on the side.

Nutritional Facts (Per Serving): Calories: 600 | Sugars: 5g | Fat: 30g | Carbs: 45g | Protein: 25g | Fiber: 5g | Sodium: 1200mg

Grilled BBQ Chicken Thighs with Corn on the Cob

Prep:10 minutes | Cook: 25 minutes | Serves: 2

Ingredients:

- 4 chicken thighs (500g)
- 1/2 cup BBQ sauce (120ml)
- 2 ears of corn (400g total)
- 1 tbsp olive oil (15ml)
- 1 tsp salt (5g)
- 1/2 tsp black pepper (2.5g)
- 1 tbsp low carb sweetener (12g)

Instructions:

1. Preheat the grill to medium-high heat.
2. Season chicken thighs with salt and black pepper. Brush with BBQ sauce.
3. Grill chicken thighs for 6-7 minutes per side, basting with BBQ sauce occasionally.
4. Brush corn with olive oil and season with salt. Grill corn for 10-12 minutes, turning occasionally, until tender and charred.
5. Serve grilled chicken thighs with corn on the cob.

Nutritional Facts (Per Serving): Calories: 600 | Sugars: 5g | Fat: 35g | Carbs: 30g | Protein: 40g | Fiber: 4g | Sodium: 1000mg

Grilled Chicken Wings with Buffalo Sauce and Celery Sticks

Prep 15 minutes | Cook: 25 minutes | Serves: 2

Ingredients:

- 12 chicken wings (500g)
- 2 tbsp olive oil (30ml)
- Salt and pepper to taste
- 1/4 cup hot sauce (60ml)
- 2 tbsp unsalted butter, melted (30g)
- 1 tsp low carb sweeteners (5g)
- 4 celery sticks (200g)

Instructions:

1. Preheat grill to medium-high heat. Toss chicken wings in olive oil, salt, and pepper.
2. Grill wings for 10-12 minutes per side, until crispy and cooked through.
3. In a small saucepan, combine hot sauce, melted butter, and low carb sweeteners. Heat until well combined.
4. Toss grilled wings in the buffalo sauce.
5. Serve wings with celery sticks on the side.

Nutritional Facts (Per Serving): Calories: 450 | Sugars: 6g | Fat: 25g | Carbohydrates: 15g | Protein: 40g | Fiber: 4g | Sodium: 10g

Grilled Lemon Herb Chicken Breasts with Quinoa Salad

Prep: 15 minutes | Cook: 25 minutes | Serves: 2

Ingredients:

- 2 chicken breasts (200g each)
- 2 tbsp olive oil (30ml)
- Juice and zest of 1 lemon
- 2 cloves garlic, minced
- 1 tsp dried oregano (1 tsp)
- Salt and pepper to taste
- 1 cup cooked quinoa (170g)
- 1 cup cherry tomatoes, halved (150g)
- 1/2 cucumber, diced (100g)
- 1/4 red onion, finely chopped (50g)
- 2 tbsp fresh parsley, chopped (8g)
- 1 tbsp olive oil (15ml)
- 1 tbsp low carb sweeteners (15ml)

Instructions:

1. Marinate chicken breasts in olive oil, lemon juice, lemon zest, garlic, oregano, salt, and pepper for at least 15 minutes.
2. Preheat grill to medium-high heat. Grill chicken for 6-7 minutes per side or until fully cooked.
3. While chicken is grilling, prepare quinoa salad by mixing cooked quinoa, cherry tomatoes, cucumber, red onion, parsley, olive oil, and low carb sweeteners in a large bowl.
4. Serve grilled chicken breasts over the quinoa salad.

Nutritional Facts (Per Serving): Calories: 600 | Sugars: 5g | Fat: 25g | Carbs: 35g | Protein: 45g | Fiber: 7g | Sodium: 600mg

Grilled Honey Mustard Chicken Drumsticks with Sweet Potato Fries

Prep: 15 minutes | Cook: 35 minutes | Serves: 2

Ingredients:

- 6 chicken drumsticks (600g)
- 1/4 cup honey (85g)
- 1/4 cup mustard (60g)
- 2 tbsp low carb sweetener (24g)
- 2 large sweet potatoes, cut into fries (400g total)
- 2 tbsp olive oil (30ml)
- 1 tsp salt (5g)
- 1/2 tsp black pepper (2.5g)
- 1 tsp paprika (5g)

Instructions:

1. Preheat grill to medium-high heat.
2. In a bowl, mix honey, mustard, and low carb sweetener. Coat drumsticks in the mixture.
3. Season sweet potato fries with olive oil, salt, black pepper, and paprika.
4. Grill drumsticks for 25-30 minutes, turning occasionally, until cooked through.
5. Grill sweet potato fries for 20-25 minutes, turning occasionally, until tender and crispy.
6. Serve grilled drumsticks with sweet potato fries.

Nutritional Facts (Per Serving): Calories: 600 | Sugars: 12g | Fat: 25g | Carbs: 50g | Protein: 30g | Fiber: 7g | Sodium: 700mg

Grilled Spicy Turkey Sausage with Bell Peppers and Onions

Prep: 15 minutes | Cook: 20 minutes | Serves: 2

Ingredients:

- 4 spicy turkey sausages (400g total)
- 2 bell peppers, sliced (300g)
- 1 large onion, sliced (150g)
- 2 tbsp olive oil (30ml)
- 1 tsp paprika (2g)
- 1 tsp garlic powder (2g)
- Salt and pepper to taste

Instructions:

1. Preheat grill to medium heat.
2. Toss bell peppers and onion with olive oil, paprika, garlic powder, salt, and pepper.
3. Grill sausages for 10-12 minutes, turning occasionally, until fully cooked.
4. Grill bell peppers and onion for 8-10 minutes, stirring occasionally, until tender and slightly charred.
5. Serve sausages with grilled bell peppers and onions.

Nutritional Facts (Per Serving): Calories: 600 | Sugars: 8g | Fat: 40g | Carbs: 30g | Protein: 25g | Fiber: 6g | Sodium: 1200mg

Grilled Turkey Thighs with Garlic and Rosemary and Roasted Carrots

Prep: 20 minutes | Cook: 40 minutes | Serves: 2

Ingredients:

- 2 turkey thighs (8 oz each) (225g each)
- 1/4 cup olive oil (60ml)
- 4 cloves garlic, minced
- 1 Tbsp fresh rosemary, chopped (15g)
- Salt and pepper to taste
- 4 large carrots, peeled and cut into sticks (400g)
- 2 Tbsp olive oil (30ml)
- 1 tsp low carb sweetener (4g)

Instructions:

1. In a bowl, mix olive oil, garlic, rosemary, salt, and pepper. Marinate turkey thighs in this mixture for 15 minutes.
2. Preheat grill to medium-high heat. Grill turkey thighs for 20-25 minutes, turning occasionally, until internal temperature reaches 165°F (74°C).
3. Preheat oven to 400°F (200°C). Toss carrots with olive oil, low carb sweetener, salt, and pepper. Spread on a baking sheet and roast for 25-30 minutes until tender and caramelized.
4. Serve grilled turkey thighs with roasted carrots.

Nutritional Facts (Per Serving): Calories: 600 | Sugars: 7g | Fat: 30g | Carbs: 40g | Protein: 35g | Fiber: 6g | Sodium: 500mg

Grilled Turkey Breast with Herb Marinade and Wild Rice Pilaf

Prep: 20 minutes | Cook: 40 minutes | Serves: 2

Ingredients:

- 2 turkey breasts (8 oz each) (225g each)
- 1/4 cup olive oil (60ml)
- 2 Tbsp lemon juice (30ml)
- 2 tsp low carb sweetener (8g)
- 2 cloves garlic, minced
- 1 Tbsp fresh rosemary, chopped (15g)
- 1 Tbsp fresh thyme, chopped (15g)
- Salt and pepper to taste
- 1 cup wild rice (185g)
- 2 cups chicken broth (480ml)
- 1 Tbsp butter (15g)

Instructions:

1. In a bowl, mix olive oil, lemon juice, low carb sweetener, garlic, rosemary, thyme, salt, and pepper. Marinate turkey breasts in this mixture for 15 minutes.
2. In a pot, bring chicken broth to a boil. Add wild rice and butter, reduce heat, cover, and simmer for 30-35 minutes until rice is tender and liquid is absorbed.
3. Preheat grill to medium-high heat. Grill turkey breasts for 6-7 minutes per side, or until internal temperature reaches 165°F (74°C).
4. Slice grilled turkey and serve over wild rice pilaf.

Nutritional Facts (Per Serving): Calories: 600 | Sugars: 2g | Fat: 20g | Carbs: 40g | Protein: 40g | Fiber: 5g | Sodium: 600mg

Grilled BBQ Turkey Legs with Macaroni and Cheese

Prep: 20 minutes | Cook: 1 hour | Serves: 2

Ingredients:

- 2 turkey legs (500g each)
- 1/2 cup BBQ sauce (120ml)
- 1 cup macaroni (100g)
- 1 cup shredded cheddar cheese (100g)
- 1 cup milk (240ml)
- 2 tbsp butter (30g)
- 2 tbsp all-purpose flour (15g)
- Salt and pepper to taste

Instructions:

1. Preheat grill to medium-high heat.
2. Coat turkey legs with BBQ sauce.
3. Grill turkey legs for 45-50 minutes, turning occasionally until cooked through.
4. Meanwhile, cook macaroni according to package instructions.
5. In a saucepan, melt butter over medium heat, stir in flour, and cook for 1 minute.
6. Gradually whisk in milk, cooking until thickened.
7. Stir in cheddar cheese until melted and smooth.
8. Combine cooked macaroni with cheese sauce, season with salt and pepper.
9. Serve grilled turkey legs with macaroni and cheese.

Nutritional Facts (Per Serving): Calories: 600 | Sugars: 6g | Fat: 30g | Carbs: 40g | Protein: 35g | Fiber: 3g | Sodium: 1000mg

Grilled Turkey Meatballs with Spaghetti Squash

Prep: 20 minutes | Cook: 40 minutes | Serves: 2

Ingredients:

- 1 lb ground turkey (450g)
- 1 large egg (60g)
- 1/4 cup grated Parmesan cheese (30g)
- 1/4 cup almond flour (30g)
- 2 tsp Italian seasoning (10g)
- 1 tsp garlic powder (5g)
- Fresh basil for garnish
- 1/2 tsp salt (2.5g)
- 1/4 tsp black pepper (1.25g)
- 1 medium spaghetti squash (1 kg)
- 2 cups marinara sauce (480ml)
- 2 tbsp olive oil (30ml)

Instructions:

1. Preheat grill to medium-high heat.
2. Halve spaghetti squash, remove seeds, brush with olive oil, season, and grill cut side down for 30-35 minutes.
3. Mix ground turkey, egg, Parmesan, almond flour, Italian seasoning, garlic powder, salt, and pepper. **Form into meatballs.**
4. Grill meatballs for 10-12 minutes, turning occasionally.
5. Heat marinara sauce in a saucepan.
6. Scrape out spaghetti squash strands with a fork.
7. Serve meatballs over spaghetti squash, topped with marinara and fresh basil.

Nutritional Facts (Per Serving): Calories: 600 | Sugars: 10g | Fat: 30g | Carbs: 30g | Protein: 50g | Fiber: 6g | Sodium: 800mg

Grilled Turkey Kabobs with Veggies and Couscous

Prep: 20 minutes | Cook: 20 minutes | Serves: 2

Ingredients:

- 1 lb turkey breast, cubed (450g)
- 1 red bell pepper, cubed (150g)
- 1 zucchini, sliced (200g)
- 1 red onion, cubed (150g)
- 2 tbsp olive oil (30ml)
- 1 tsp dried oregano (2g)
- 1 tsp paprika (2g)
- Salt and pepper to taste
- 1 cup couscous (180g)
- 1 1/4 cups chicken broth (300ml)
- 2 tbsp chopped fresh parsley (10g)

Instructions:

1. Preheat grill to medium-high heat.
2. In a bowl, combine turkey, bell pepper, zucchini, and onion with olive oil, oregano, paprika, salt, and pepper. Thread onto skewers.
3. Grill kabobs for 12-15 minutes, turning occasionally, until turkey is cooked through.
4. Meanwhile, bring chicken broth to a boil. Stir in couscous, cover, and remove from heat. Let sit for 5 minutes, then fluff with a fork and mix in parsley.
5. Serve grilled turkey kabobs over couscous.

Nutritional Facts (Per Serving): Calories: 600 | Sugars: 6g | Fat: 20g | Carbs: 50g | Protein: 40g | Fiber: 5g | Sodium: 800mg

CHAPTER 12: LUNCHES: Pork

Grilled Pork Chops with Apple Glaze and Sautéed Spinach

Prep: 15 minutes | Cook: 25 minutes | Serves: 2

Ingredients:

- 2 bone-in pork chops (250g each)
- 1/2 cup apple juice (120ml)
- 1 tbsp low carb sweetener (15g)
- 1 tbsp Dijon mustard (15g)
- 1 tsp apple cider vinegar (5ml)
- 1 tbsp olive oil (15ml)
- 1 garlic clove, minced (5g)
- 8 cups fresh spinach (240g)
- Salt and pepper to taste

Instructions:

1. Preheat grill to medium-high heat.
2. Season pork chops with salt and pepper, grill for 4-5 minutes per side.
3. Simmer apple juice, sweetener, Dijon mustard, and apple cider vinegar until reduced by half, 5-7 minutes.
4. Brush apple glaze on pork chops during the last 2 minutes of grilling.
5. Sauté garlic in olive oil, add spinach and cook until wilted, 3-4 minutes. Season with salt and pepper. Serve pork chops with sautéed spinach.

Nutritional Facts (Per Serving): Calories: 600 | Sugars: 8g | Fat: 25g | Carbs: 20g | Protein: 65g | Fiber: 5g | Sodium: 600mg

Grilled Pork Tenderloin with Herb Rub and Roasted Sweet Potatoes

Prep: 15 minutes | Cook: 30 minutes | Serves: 2

Ingredients:

- 1 lb pork tenderloin (450g)
- 1 tbsp olive oil (15ml)
- 1 tsp garlic powder (5g)
- 1 tsp dried thyme (5g)
- 1 tsp dried rosemary (5g)
- Salt and pepper to taste
- 2 medium sweet potatoes, diced (400g)
- 1 tbsp olive oil (15ml)
- 1 tsp smoked paprika (5g)

Instructions:

1. Preheat grill to medium-high heat. Rub pork tenderloin with olive oil, garlic powder, thyme, rosemary, salt, and pepper.
2. Grill pork tenderloin for 20-25 minutes, turning occasionally, until internal temperature reaches 145°F (63°C). Let rest 5 minutes before slicing.
3. Preheat oven to 400°F (200°C). Toss diced sweet potatoes with olive oil, smoked paprika, salt, and pepper. Roast on a baking sheet for 20-25 min.
4. Serve sliced pork tenderloin with roasted sweet potatoes.

Nutritional Facts (Per Serving): Calories: 600 | Sugars: 8g | Fat: 20g | Carbs: 50g | Protein: 40g | Fiber: 8g | Sodium: 600mg

Grilled BBQ Pulled Pork with Coleslaw and Cornbread

Prep: 20 minutes | Cook: 6 hours | Serves: 2

Ingredients:

- 1 lb pork shoulder (450g)
- 1/2 cup BBQ sauce (120ml)
- 2 tbsp low carb sweeteners (20g)
- 1/4 cup apple cider vinegar (60ml)
- 1/4 cup Greek yogurt (60g)
- 2 cups shredded cabbage (150g)
- 1 carrot, shredded (50g)
- 1 tbsp apple cider vinegar (15ml)
- Salt and pepper to taste
- 1/2 cup cornmeal (70g)
- 1/2 cup flour (60g)
- 1/4 cup milk (60ml)
- 1 egg

Instructions:

1. Preheat grill to medium heat. Season pork shoulder with salt and pepper.

2. Grill pork over indirect heat for 5-6 hours, basting with BBQ sauce every hour, until tender.

3. Mix sweetener, apple cider vinegar, shredded cabbage, carrot, and Greek yogurt for coleslaw. Season with salt and pepper.

4. Preheat oven to 375°F (190°C). Mix cornmeal, flour, milk, and egg. Bake in a greased dish for 20-25 minutes.

5. Shred pork, mix with remaining BBQ sauce. Serve with coleslaw and cornbread.

Nutritional Facts (Per Serving): Calories: 600 | Sugars: 10g | Fat: 30g | Carbs: 40g | Protein: 30g | Fiber: 5g | Sodium: 800mg

Grilled Pork Belly with Honey Soy Glaze and Stir-Fried Vegetables

Prep: 15 minutes | Cook: 30 minutes | Serves: 2

Ingredients:

- 1 lb pork belly (450g)
- 2 tbsp soy sauce (30ml)
- 1 tbsp honey (15ml)
- 1 tbsp low carb sweeteners (15ml)
- 1 tbsp rice vinegar (15ml)
- 1 tsp sesame oil (5ml)
- 2 cups mixed vegetables (bell peppers, carrots, broccoli) (300g)
- 2 tbsp vegetable oil (30ml)
- Salt and pepper to taste

Instructions:

1. Preheat grill to medium-high heat.

2. In a bowl, mix soy sauce, honey, low carb sweeteners, rice vinegar, and sesame oil. Marinate pork belly in the mixture for 10 minutes.

3. Grill pork belly for 6-8 minutes per side, basting with the glaze, until cooked through and caramelized.

4. In a large skillet, heat vegetable oil over medium-high heat. Add mixed vegetables and stir-fry for 5-7 minutes until tender. Season with salt and pepper.. Slice the grilled pork belly and serve with stir-fried vegetables.

Nutritional Facts (Per Serving): Calories: 600 | Sugars: 8g | Fat: 40g | Carbs: 20g | Protein: 35g | Fiber: 4g | Sodium: 1200mg

Grilled Pork Sausages with Onions and German Potato Salad

Prep: 15 minutes | Cook: 25 minutes | Serves: 2

Ingredients:

- 4 pork sausages (500g)
- 1 large onion, sliced (200g)
- 1 lb potatoes, peeled and cubed (450g)
- 2 tbsp olive oil (30ml)
- 2 tbsp white vinegar (30ml)
- 1 tbsp low carb sweeteners
- 1 tsp mustard (5ml)
- 2 tbsp fresh parsley, chopped (10g)
- Salt and pepper to taste

Instructions:

1. Preheat grill to medium-high heat. Grill sausages for 10-12 minutes, turning occasionally.
2. Heat olive oil in a pan, cook sliced onions until caramelized, about 10 minutes.
3. Boil cubed potatoes until tender, about 10 minutes. Drain and cool.
4. Whisk olive oil, vinegar, sweeteners, mustard, salt, and pepper. Toss potatoes with dressing and parsley.
5. Serve grilled sausages with caramelized onions and German potato salad.

Nutritional Facts (Per Serving): Calories: 600 | Sugars: 5g | Fat: 40g | Carbs: 20g | Protein: 20g | Fiber: 3g | Sodium: 1200mg

Grilled Pork Loin with Mustard Sauce and Green Bean Almondine

Prep: 15 minutes | Cook: 25 minutes | Serves: 2

Ingredients:

- 1 lb pork loin (450g)
- 2 tbsp Dijon mustard (30ml)
- 1 tbsp low carb sweeteners (15ml)
- 1 tbsp apple cider vinegar (15ml)
- 1 tsp garlic powder (5g)
- 2 cups green beans (200g)
- 2 tbsp sliced almonds (30g)
- 2 tbsp butter (30g)
- 1 tbsp olive oil (15ml)
- Salt and pepper to taste

Instructions:

1. Preheat grill to medium-high heat.
2. In a small bowl, mix Dijon mustard, low carb sweeteners, apple cider vinegar, and garlic powder. Spread the mixture over the pork loin.
3. Grill pork loin for 25-30 minutes, turning occasionally, until the internal temperature reaches 145°F (63°C).
4. In a large skillet, heat butter and olive oil over medium heat. Add green beans and cook for 5-7 minutes until tender. Add sliced almonds and cook for an additional 2 minutes. Season with salt and pepper.
5. Slice the grilled pork loin and serve with green bean almondine.

Nutritional Facts (Per Serving): Calories: 600 | Sugars: 4g | Fat: 36g | Carbs: 12g | Protein: 50g | Fiber: 4g | Sodium: 800mg

Grilled Pork Chops with Apple Glaze and Sautéed Spinach

Prep: 15 minutes | Cook: 25 minutes | Serves: 2

Ingredients:

- 1 lb beef sirloin, cut into cubes (450g)
- 2 bell peppers, cut into chunks (300g)
- 1 tbsp olive oil (15ml)
- 1 tsp ground cumin (5g)
- 1 tsp smoked paprika (5g)
- 1 cup basmati rice (200g)
- 2 cups water (480ml)
- 1 tsp ground turmeric (5g)
- 1 tbsp low carb sweeteners (15ml)
- Salt and pepper to taste

Instructions:

1. Preheat grill to medium-high heat.
2. Mix beef cubes with olive oil, cumin, smoked paprika, salt, and pepper. Thread beef and bell peppers onto skewers.
3. Grill kebabs for 8-10 minutes, turning occasionally.
4. Boil water, add basmati rice, turmeric, sweeteners, and salt. Simmer for 15 minutes until tender.
5. Serve grilled beef kebabs with turmeric rice.

Nutritional Facts (Per Serving): Calories: 600 | Sugars: 4g | Fat: 25g | Carbs: 50g | Protein: 35g | Fiber: 4g | Sodium: 600mg

Grilled Beef Tenderloin with Garlic and Herb Roasted Potatoes

Prep: 20 minutes | Cook: 30 minutes | Serves: 2

Ingredients:

- 12 oz beef tenderloin (340g)
- 1 lb baby potatoes, halved (450g)
- 2 tbsp olive oil (30ml)
- 4 cloves garlic, minced (20g)
- 1 tbsp fresh rosemary, chopped (15g)
- 1 tbsp fresh thyme, chopped (15g)
- 1 tsp salt (5g)
- 1 tsp black pepper (5g)
- 1 tbsp lemon juice (15ml)
- Fresh parsley, chopped for garnish

Instructions:

1. Preheat grill to medium-high heat.
Toss potatoes with olive oil, garlic, rosemary, thyme, salt, and pepper. Roast at 400°F (200°C) for 20-25 minutes.
Rub beef tenderloin with olive oil, salt, and pepper. Grill for 4-5 minutes per side for medium-rare.
Let beef rest for 5 minutes, then slice.
Serve sliced beef tenderloin with roasted potatoes, garnished with parsley.

Nutritional Facts (Per Serving): Calories: 600 | Sugars: 4g | Fat: 30g | Carbs: 50g | Protein: 35g | Fiber: 5g | Sodium: 700mg

Grilled Beef and Veggie Stir-Fry with Jasmine Rice

Prep: 20 minutes | Cook: 20 minutes | Serves: 2

Ingredients:

- 8 oz beef sirloin, thinly sliced (225g)
- 1 cup jasmine rice, cooked (190g)
- 1 bell pepper, sliced (150g)
- 1 zucchini, sliced (200g)
- 1 cup broccoli florets (150g)
- 2 tbsp soy sauce (30ml)
- 1 tbsp low carb sweetener (15g)
- 2 tsp sesame oil (10ml)
- 2 cloves garlic, minced
- 1 tsp fresh ginger, grated (5g)
- 2 green onions, sliced
- 1 tbsp sesame seeds (15g)
- Salt and pepper to taste

Instructions:

1. Heat sesame oil in a grill pan over medium-high heat.
2. Add garlic and ginger, sauté for 1 minute until fragrant.
3. Add beef slices and cook until browned, about 3-4 minutes.
4. Add bell pepper, zucchini, and broccoli, stir-fry for 5-6 minutes until vegetables are tender.
5. Stir in soy sauce and low carb sweetener, cook for an additional 2 minutes.
6. Serve stir-fry over jasmine rice, garnish with green onions and sesame seeds.

Nutritional Facts (Per Serving): Calories: 600 | Sugars: 5g | Fat: 20g | Carbs: 65g | Protein: 35g | Fiber: 5g | Sodium: 1200mg

Grilled Teriyaki Beef with Steamed Broccoli and Rice Noodles

Prep: 15 minutes | Cook: 30 minutes | Serves: 2

Ingredients:

- 1 lb beef sirloin (450g)
- 1/4 cup teriyaki sauce (60ml)
- 1 tbsp olive oil (15ml)
- 2 cups broccoli florets (300g)
- 4 oz rice noodles (120g)
- 1 tbsp low carb sweetener (15g)
- 1 clove garlic, minced
- 1 tsp sesame oil (5ml)
- Salt and pepper to taste

Instructions:

1. Cut the beef sirloin into strips. In a bowl, combine beef, teriyaki sauce, olive oil, low carb sweetener, and minced garlic. Let marinate for 10 minutes.
2. Heat a grill pan over medium-high heat. Grill beef strips for 2-3 minutes on each side until cooked to desired doneness. Remove from pan and set aside.
3. In a steamer, cook broccoli florets until tender, about 5-6 minutes.
4. Cook rice noodles according to package instructions. Drain and toss with sesame oil.
5. Plate rice noodles, top with grilled beef and steamed broccoli. Season with salt and pepper to taste.

Nutritional Facts (Per Serving): Calories: 600 | Sugars: 8g | Fat: 22g | Carbs: 52g | Protein: 42g | Fiber: 6g | Sodium: 1500mg

Grilled Stuffed Jalapeños with Cream Cheese

Prep: 10 minutes | Cook: 10 minutes | Serves: 2

Ingredients:

- 6 jalapeños, halved and seeded
- 8 oz cream cheese (225g)
- 1/2 cup shredded cheddar cheese (60g)
- 1/4 tsp garlic powder (1g)
- 1/4 tsp onion powder (1g)
- 1/4 tsp smoked paprika (1g)

Instructions:

1. Preheat grill to medium-high heat.
2. In a bowl, mix cream cheese, cheddar cheese, garlic powder, onion powder, and smoked paprika.
3. Stuff each jalapeño half with the cheese mixture.
4. Grill stuffed jalapeños until the cheese is melted and the jalapeños are slightly charred, about 8-10 minutes.
5. Serve immediately.

Nutritional Facts (Per Serving): Calories: 400 | Carbs: 8g | Protein: 8g | Fat: 36g | Fiber: 2g | Sodium: 500mg | Sugars: 5g

Grilled Artichoke Hearts with Lemon Aioli

Prep: 15 minutes | Cook: 10 minutes | Serves: 2

Ingredients:

- 6 artichoke hearts, halved
- 2 tbsp olive oil (30ml)
- 1/2 tsp salt (2g)
- 1/2 tsp black pepper (2g)
- 1/2 cup Greek yogurt (120g)
- 1 tbsp lemon juice (15ml)
- 1 clove garlic, minced

Instructions:

1. Preheat grill to medium heat.
2. Brush artichoke hearts with olive oil and season with salt and pepper.
3. Grill artichoke hearts until tender and slightly charred, about 5 minutes per side.
4. In a bowl, mix Greek yogurt, lemon juice, and minced garlic to make the aioli.
5. Serve grilled artichoke hearts with lemon aioli.

Nutritional Facts (Per Serving): Calories: 400 | Carbs: 12g | Protein: 8g | Fat: 32g | Fiber: 6g | Sodium: 700mg | Sugars: 3g

Grilled Avocado Halves with Salsa

Prep: 10 minutes | Cook: 5 minutes | Serves: 2

Ingredients:

- 2 avocados, halved and pitted
- 1 tbsp olive oil (15ml)
- 1/2 cup cherry tomatoes, diced (80g)
- 1/4 cup red onion, diced (40g)
- 1 tbsp cilantro, chopped (15g)
- 1 tbsp lime juice (15ml)
- 1/4 tsp salt (1g)
- 1/4 tsp black pepper (1g)

Instructions:

1. Preheat grill to medium-high heat.
2. Brush avocado halves with olive oil.
3. Grill avocados, cut side down, until grill marks appear, about 3-5 minutes.
4. In a bowl, mix cherry tomatoes, red onion, cilantro, lime juice, salt, and black pepper to make the salsa.
5. Spoon salsa into grilled avocado halves and serve.

Nutritional Facts (Per Serving): Calories: 400 | Carbs: 16g | Protein: 5g | Fat: 36g | Fiber: 12g | Sodium: 350mg | Sugars: 5g

Grilled Halloumi Cheese with Lemon

Prep: 5 minutes | Cook: 5 minutes | Serves: 2

Ingredients:

- 8 oz halloumi cheese, sliced (225g)
- 1 tbsp olive oil (15ml)
- 1 lemon, cut into wedges

Instructions:

1. Preheat grill to medium-high heat.
2. Brush halloumi slices with olive oil.
3. Grill halloumi until golden brown, about 2-3 minutes per side.
4. Serve grilled halloumi with lemon wedges.

Nutritional Facts (Per Serving): Calories: 400 | Carbs: 4g | Protein: 22g | Fat: 32g | Fiber: 0g | Sodium: 800mg | Sugars: 1g

Smoky Grilled Eggplant Dip

Prep: 10 minutes | Cook: 20 minutes | Serves: 2

Ingredients:

- 1 large eggplant (400g)
- 2 tbsp olive oil (30ml)
- 2 cloves garlic, minced
- 1/2 cup Greek yogurt (120g)
- 1 tsp smoked paprika (2g)
- 1/2 tsp salt (2g)
- 1/2 tsp black pepper (2g)
- 1 tbsp lemon juice (15ml)

Instructions:

1. Preheat grill to medium-high heat.
2. Brush eggplant with olive oil and grill until charred and tender, about 20 minutes.
3. Scoop out eggplant flesh and blend with garlic, Greek yogurt, smoked paprika, salt, black pepper, and lemon juice until smooth.
4. Serve with pita or veggies.

Nutritional Facts (Per Serving): Calories: 400 | Carbs: 20g | Protein: 6g | Fat: 34g | Fiber: 8g | Sodium: 600mg | Sugars: 10g

Grilled Artichoke Spinach Dip

Prep: 15 minutes | Cook: 10 minutes | Serves: 2

Ingredients:

- 6 artichoke hearts, halved (200g)
- 1 cup fresh spinach, chopped (30g)
- 1/2 cup Greek yogurt (120g)
- 1/2 cup grated Parmesan cheese (50g)
- 1 tbsp olive oil (15ml)
- 1 clove garlic, minced
- 1/2 tsp salt (2g)
- 1/4 tsp black pepper (1g)

Instructions:

1. Preheat grill to medium heat.
2. Brush artichoke hearts with olive oil and grill until tender, about 5 minutes per side.
3. Mix grilled artichoke hearts with spinach, Greek yogurt, Parmesan cheese, garlic, salt, and pepper.
4. Serve warm.

Nutritional Facts (Per Serving): Calories: 400 | Carbs: 14g | Protein: 18g | Fat: 30g | Fiber: 8g | Sodium: 700mg | Sugars: 4g

Grilled Avocado and Mango Salsa

Prep: 10 minutes | Cook: 5 minutes | Serves: 2

Ingredients:

- 2 avocados, halved and pitted
- 1 mango, diced (200g)
- 1/4 cup red onion, diced (40g)
- 1 tbsp cilantro, chopped (15g)
- 1 tbsp lime juice (15ml)
- 1 tbsp olive oil (15ml)
- 1/4 tsp salt (1g)
- 1/4 tsp black pepper (1g)

Instructions:

1. Preheat grill to medium-high heat.
2. Brush avocado halves with olive oil.
3. Grill avocados, cut side down, until grill marks appear, about 3-5 minutes.
4. Scoop out grilled avocado flesh and mix with mango, red onion, cilantro, lime juice, salt, and black pepper.
5. Serve as a dip or topping.

Nutritional Facts (Per Serving): Calories: 400 | Carbs: 36g | Protein: 4g | Fat: 30g | Fiber: 12g | Sodium: 200mg | Sugars: 18g

Grilled Jalapeño and Lime Hummus

Prep: 10 minutes | Cook: 10 minutes | Serves: 2

Ingredients:

- 1 cup canned chickpeas, drained and rinsed (240g)
- 2 jalapeños, halved and seeded
- 2 tbsp olive oil (30ml)
- 2 tbsp tahini (30g)
- 1 clove garlic, minced
- 1 tbsp lime juice (15ml)
- 1/2 tsp salt (2g)
- 1/4 tsp cumin (1g)

Instructions:

1. Preheat grill to medium-high heat.
2. Brush jalapeños with olive oil and grill until charred, about 5 minutes per side.
3. Blend chickpeas, grilled jalapeños, tahini, garlic, lime juice, salt, cumin, and remaining olive oil until smooth.
4. Serve with pita or veggies.

Nutritional Facts (Per Serving): Calories: 400 | Carbs: 30g | Protein: 10g | Fat: 28g | Fiber: 10g | Sodium: 600mg | Sugars: 2g

Grilled Lemon Pound Cake with Berries

Prep: 10 minutes | Cook: 5 minutes | Serves: 2

Ingredients:

- 4 slices lemon pound cake (200g)
- 1 tbsp butter, melted (15g)
- 1 cup mixed berries (150g)
- 1 tbsp honey (20g)

Instructions:

1. Preheat grill to medium heat.
2. Brush pound cake slices with melted butter.
3. Grill pound cake until golden and slightly charred, about 2-3 minutes per side.
4. Serve grilled pound cake with mixed berries and a drizzle of honey.

Nutritional Facts (Per Serving): Calories: 400 | Carbs: 60g | Protein: 4g | Fat: 16g | Fiber: 4g | Sodium: 220mg | Sugars: 40g

Grilled Pear and Blue Cheese Spread

Prep: 10 minutes | Cook: 5 minutes | Serves: 2

Ingredients:

- pears, halved and cored (300g)
- 2 tbsp olive oil (30ml)
- 1/2 cup crumbled blue cheese (60g)
- 1 tbsp honey (20g)
- 1 tbsp chopped walnuts (15g)

Instructions:

1. Preheat grill to medium-high heat.
2. Brush pear halves with olive oil.
3. Grill pears until tender and grill marks appear, about 3-5 minutes per side.
4. Top grilled pears with blue cheese, honey, and chopped walnuts.

Nutritional Facts (Per Serving): Calories: 400 | Carbs: 40g | Protein: 8g | Fat: 24g | Fiber: 6g | Sodium: 300mg | Sugars: 30g

Grilled Blueberry Crisp

Prep: 10 minutes | Cook: 10 minutes | Serves: 2

Ingredients:

- 1 cup blueberries (150g)
- 1 tbsp honey (20g)
- 1/4 cup rolled oats (30g)
- 2 tbsp almond flour (15g)
- 2 tbsp butter, melted (30g)
- 1/4 tsp cinnamon (1g)

Instructions:

1. Preheat grill to medium heat.
2. In a bowl, mix blueberries with honey.
3. In another bowl, mix oats, almond flour, melted butter, and cinnamon.
4. Divide blueberries between two foil packets and top with oat mixture.
5. Grill packets until blueberries are bubbly and topping is golden, about 10 minutes.
6. Serve warm.

Nutritional Facts (Per Serving): Calories: 400 | Carbs: 50g | Protein: 6g | Fat: 20g | Fiber: 8g | Sodium: 60mg | Sugars: 30g

Grilled Coconut Macaroons

Prep: 10 minutes | Cook: 10 minutes | Serves: 2

Ingredients:

- 1 cup shredded coconut (80g)
- 1/4 cup low carb sweeteners (50g)
- 1/2 tsp vanilla extract (2ml)
- 1/4 tsp salt (1g)
- 2 egg whites

Instructions:

1. Preheat grill to medium heat.
2. In a bowl, mix shredded coconut, low carb sweeteners, egg whites, vanilla extract, and salt.
3. Form mixture into small mounds and place on a greased grill-safe tray.
4. Grill macaroons until golden and set, about 8-10 minutes.
5. Serve cooled.

Nutritional Facts (Per Serving): Calories: 400 | Carbs: 18g | Protein: 6g | Fat: 36g | Fiber: 8g | Sodium: 140mg | Sugars: 10g

Grilled Pumpkin Pie Slices

Prep: 10 minutes | Cook: 10 minutes | Serves: 2

Ingredients:

- 4 slices pumpkin pie (200g)
- 2 tbsp melted butter (30g)
- 1 tsp cinnamon (2g)
- 1 tbsp low carb sweeteners (15g)

Instructions:

1. Preheat grill to medium heat.
2. Brush pumpkin pie slices with melted butter.
3. Sprinkle with cinnamon and low carb sweeteners.
4. Grill slices until slightly caramelized and heated through, about 3-5 minutes per side.
5. Serve warm.

Nutritional Facts (Per Serving): Calories: 400 | Carbs: 40g | Protein: 6g | Fat: 26g | Fiber: 4g | Sodium: 300mg | Sugars: 20g

Grilled Cheesecake with Berry Compote

Prep: 10 minutes | Cook: 10 minutes | Serves: 2

Ingredients:

- 4 slices cheesecake (200g)
- 1 cup mixed berries (150g)
- 1 tbsp honey (20g)
- 1 tsp lemon juice (5ml)
- 2 tbsp Greek yogurt (30g)

Instructions:

1. Preheat grill to medium heat.
2. Grill cheesecake slices until lightly charred and warmed through, about 2-3 minutes per side.
3. In a small saucepan, heat berries, honey, and lemon juice over medium heat until berries are soft and sauce thickens, about 5 minutes.
4. Serve grilled cheesecake with berry compote and a dollop of Greek yogurt.

Nutritional Facts (Per Serving): Calories: 400 | Carbs: 40g | Protein: 8g | Fat: 24g | Fiber: 4g | Sodium: 200mg | Sugars: 25g

CHAPTER 17: DINNER: Low Fat & Low Calorie Options

Grilled Lemon Herb Chicken Breasts with Steamed Broccoli

Prep: 10 minutes | Cook: 20 minutes | Serves: 2

Ingredients:

- 2 chicken breasts (each 200g)
- 1 lemon, juice and zest
- 2 tbsp olive oil (30ml)
- 1 tsp garlic powder (5g)
- 1 tsp dried thyme (5g)
- 1 tsp dried rosemary (5g)
- Salt and pepper to taste
- 2 cups broccoli florets (300g)

Instructions:

1. In a bowl, mix lemon juice, lemon zest, olive oil, garlic powder, thyme, rosemary, salt, and pepper. Marinate chicken breasts for 10 minutes.
2. Preheat grill to medium heat. Grill chicken breasts for 6-7 minutes per side or until fully cooked.
3. Meanwhile, steam broccoli until tender, about 5-7 minutes.
4. Serve grilled chicken with steamed broccoli.

Nutritional Facts (Per Serving): Calories: 400 | Sugars: 2g | Fat: 20g | Carbs: 12g | Protein: 45g | Fiber: 4g | Sodium: 200mg

Grilled Turkey Burgers with Spinach and Feta

Prep: 15 minutes | Cook: 10 minutes | Serves: 2

Ingredients:

- 1 lb ground turkey (450g)
- 1 cup fresh spinach, chopped (30g)
- 1/2 cup feta cheese, crumbled (75g)
- 1 egg (50g)
- 1/4 cup breadcrumbs (30g)
- 1 tsp garlic powder (5g)
- 1 tsp onion powder (5g)
- Salt and pepper to taste
- 2 whole wheat burger buns (120g total)
- 1 tbsp olive oil (15ml)

Instructions:

1. Combine ground turkey, spinach, feta, egg, breadcrumbs, garlic powder, onion powder, salt, and pepper. Form into 2 patties.
2. Preheat grill to medium-high heat and brush grates with olive oil.
3. Grill patties for 5-6 minutes per side until fully cooked. Serve on whole wheat buns.

Nutritional Information (Per Serving): Calories: 400 | Sugars: 2g | Fat: 20g | Carbohydrates: 22g | Protein: 35g | Fiber: 4g | Sodium: 600mg

Grilled Chicken and Vegetable Skewers with Quinoa

Prep: 20 minutes | Cook: 15 minutes | Serves: 2

Ingredients:

- 2 chicken breasts, cubed (400g)
- 1 red bell pepper, diced (150g)
- 1 zucchini, sliced (200g)
- 1 red onion, quartered (150g)
- 2 tbsp olive oil (30ml)
- 2 tsp garlic powder (10g)
- 2 tsp dried oregano (10g)
- Salt and pepper to taste
- 1 cup quinoa (170g)
- 2 cups water (480ml)

Instructions:

1. Preheat grill to medium-high heat. In a bowl, mix olive oil, garlic powder, oregano, salt, and pepper. Marinate chicken and vegetables in the mixture for 10 minutes.
2. Thread chicken and vegetables onto skewers.
3. Grill skewers for 10-12 minutes, turning occasionally, until chicken is fully cooked.
4. Meanwhile, cook quinoa in water as per package instructions.
5. Serve grilled skewers over cooked quinoa.

Nutritional Facts (Per Serving): Calories: 400 | Sugars: 5g | Fat: 14g | Carbs: 35g | Protein: 35g | Fiber: 6g | Sodium: 300mg

Grilled Portobello Mushrooms with Garlic and Thyme

Prep: 10 minutes | Cook: 15 minutes | Serves: 2

Ingredients:

- 4 large portobello mushrooms (400g)
- 2 tbsp olive oil (30ml)
- 2 cloves garlic, minced (10g)
- 2 tsp fresh thyme leaves (10g)
- Salt and pepper to taste

Instructions:

1. Preheat grill to medium-high heat. In a small bowl, mix olive oil, minced garlic, thyme leaves, salt, and pepper.
2. Brush the mixture onto both sides of the portobello mushrooms.
3. Grill mushrooms for 5-7 minutes per side, until tender and slightly charred.
4. Serve hot as a main dish or side.

Nutritional Facts (Per Serving): Calories: 400 | Sugars: 4g | Fat: 30g | Carbs: 20g | Protein: 8g | Fiber: 6g | Sodium: 200mg

Grilled Zucchini Boats with Lean Turkey and Marinara

Prep: 15 minutes | Cook: 20 minutes | Serves: 2

Ingredients:

- 2 large zucchinis, halved lengthwise (400g)
- 8 oz lean ground turkey (225g)
- 1 cup marinara sauce (240ml)
- 1/2 cup shredded mozzarella cheese (60g)
- 1 tbsp olive oil (15ml)
- 2 cloves garlic, minced (10g)
- 1 tsp dried oregano (5g)
- Salt and pepper to taste

Instructions:

1. Preheat grill to medium-high heat. Scoop out the center of each zucchini half to create boats.
2. In a skillet, heat olive oil over medium heat. Add garlic and cook for 1 minute. Add ground turkey, oregano, salt, and pepper. Cook until turkey is browned, about 5-7 minutes.
3. Mix in marinara sauce and cook for another 2 minutes.
4. Fill zucchini boats with the turkey mixture. Top with shredded mozzarella.
5. Place zucchini boats on the grill, cover, and cook for 10-12 minutes, until zucchini is tender and cheese is melted.

Nutritional Facts (Per Serving): Calories: 400 | Sugars: 6g | Fat: 20g | Carbs: 18g | Protein: 34g | Fiber: 4g | Sodium: 600mg

Grilled Eggplant Parmesan with Fresh Basil

Prep: 15 minutes | Cook: 20 minutes | Serves: 2

Ingredients:

- 1 large eggplant, sliced into rounds (300g)
- 2 tbsp olive oil (30ml)
- 1 cup marinara sauce (240ml)
- 1/2 cup shredded mozzarella cheese (60g)
- 1/4 cup grated Parmesan cheese (30g)
- Fresh basil leaves for garnish (10g)
- Salt and pepper to taste

Instructions:

1. Preheat grill to medium-high heat. Brush eggplant slices with olive oil and season with salt and pepper.
2. Grill eggplant slices for 5-7 minutes per side, until tender and grill marks appear.
3. Spread a layer of marinara sauce on each grilled eggplant slice. Top with mozzarella and Parmesan cheese.
4. Close the grill lid and cook for an additional 2-3 minutes, until cheese is melted and bubbly.
5. Garnish with fresh basil leaves and serve hot.

Nutritional Facts (Per Serving): Calories: 400 | Sugars: 7g | Fat: 28g | Carbs: 22g | Protein: 15g | Fiber: 8g | Sodium: 600mg

Grilled Cod Fillet with Lemon Dill Sauce and Asparagus

Prep: 15 minutes | Cook: 15 minutes | Serves: 2

Ingredients:

- 2 cod fillets (300g each)
- 1 bunch asparagus, trimmed (250g)
- 2 tbsp olive oil (30ml)
- Salt and pepper to taste
- 1 lemon, juice and zest
- 1/4 cup Greek yogurt (60g)
- 1 tbsp fresh dill, chopped (15g)
- 1 clove garlic, minced (5g)

Instructions:

1. Preheat grill to medium-high heat. Brush cod fillets and asparagus with olive oil, and season with salt and pepper.
2. Grill cod fillets for 4-5 minutes per side, until cooked through and opaque.
3. Grill asparagus for 5-7 minutes, turning occasionally, until tender.
4. In a small bowl, mix lemon juice, lemon zest, Greek yogurt, dill, and minced garlic to make the sauce.
5. Serve grilled cod with asparagus, drizzling the lemon dill sauce over the top.

Nutritional Facts (Per Serving): Calories: 400 | Sugars: 3g | Fat: 18g | Carbs: 10g | Protein: 50g | Fiber: 4g | Sodium: 300mg

Grilled Chicken Caesar Salad with Light Dressing

Prep: 15 minutes | Cook: 15 minutes | Serves: 2

Ingredients:

- 2 boneless, skinless chicken breasts (8 oz each) (230g)
- 1 tbsp olive oil (15ml)
- Salt and pepper to taste
- 4 cups romaine lettuce, chopped (200g)
- 1/4 cup grated Parmesan cheese (25g)
- 1/2 cup cherry tomatoes, halved (100g)
- 1/2 cup croutons (50g)
- 2 tbsp Caesar dressing (30ml)
- 1 tsp low carb sweeteners (5g)

Instructions:

1. Preheat grill to medium-high heat. Brush chicken breasts with olive oil and season with salt and pepper.
2. Grill chicken for 6-7 minutes per side, until fully cooked. Let rest for 5 minutes, then slice thinly.
3. In a large bowl, toss romaine lettuce with Parmesan cheese, cherry tomatoes, and croutons.
4. Add sliced chicken to the salad and drizzle with Caesar dressing. Sprinkle low carb sweeteners on top.

Nutritional Facts (Per Serving): Calories: 400 | Sugars: 4g | Fat: 20g | Carbs: 12g | Protein: 36g | Fiber: 3g | Sodium: 800mg

Grilled Tilapia with Mango Salsa and Wild Rice

Prep: 15 minutes | Cook: 20 minutes | Serves: 2

Ingredients:

- 2 tilapia fillets (6 oz each) (170g)
- 1 tbsp olive oil (15ml)
- Salt and pepper to taste
- 1 cup cooked wild rice (200g)
- 1/2 cup diced mango (75g)
- 1/4 cup diced red onion (40g)
- 1/4 cup diced red bell pepper (40g)
- 1 tbsp chopped fresh cilantro (15g)
- Juice of 1 lime (15ml)
- 1 tsp low carb sweeteners (5g)

Instructions:

1. Preheat grill to medium-high heat. Brush tilapia fillets with olive oil and season with salt and pepper.
2. Grill tilapia for 3-4 minutes per side, until fully cooked.
3. In a bowl, combine diced mango, red onion, red bell pepper, cilantro, lime juice, and low carb sweeteners to make the salsa.
4. Serve grilled tilapia with mango salsa on top and wild rice on the side.

Nutritional Facts (Per Serving): Calories: 400 | Sugars: 6g | Fat: 12g | Carbs: 30g | Protein: 30g | Fiber: 4g | Sodium: 300mg

Grilled Eggplant and Tomato Stack

Prep: 15 minutes | Cook: 20 minutes | Serves: 2

Ingredients:

- 1 large eggplant, sliced (1 lb) (450g)
- 2 large tomatoes, sliced (1 lb) (450g)
- 2 tbsp olive oil (30ml)
- Salt and pepper to taste
- 1/4 cup crumbled feta cheese (30g)
- 1/4 cup chopped fresh basil (15g)
- 1 tbsp balsamic vinegar (15ml)

Instructions:

1. Preheat grill to medium-high heat. Brush eggplant and tomato slices with olive oil and season with salt and pepper.
2. Grill eggplant slices for 4-5 minutes per side, until tender and grill-marked. Grill tomato slices for 2-3 minutes per side, until slightly charred.
3. Stack grilled eggplant and tomato slices alternately on plates, sprinkling each layer with feta cheese and basil.
4. Drizzle balsamic vinegar over the top and serve immediately.

Nutritional Facts (Per Serving): Calories: 400 | Sugars: 10g | Fat: 26g | Carbs: 34g | Protein: 7g | Fiber: 14g | Sodium: 500mg

CHAPTER 18: DINNER: Hearty Salads with Grilled Proteins

Grilled Pork Tenderloin Salad with Apples and Pecans

Prep: 20 minutes | Cook: 15 minutes | Serves: 2

Ingredients:

- 1 lb pork tenderloin (450g)
- 1 tbsp olive oil (15ml)
- Salt and pepper to taste
- 2 cups mixed salad greens (100g)
- 1 apple, thinly sliced (150g)
- 1/4 cup pecans, toasted (30g)
- 2 tbsp crumbled goat cheese (30g)
- 2 tbsp balsamic vinaigrette

Instructions:

1. Preheat grill to medium-high heat. Rub pork tenderloin with olive oil, salt, and pepper.
2. Grill pork for 7-8 minutes per side until internal temperature reaches 145°F (63°C). Let rest 5 minutes, then slice.
3. Combine salad greens, apple slices, pecans, and goat cheese in a bowl.
4. Top salad with sliced pork and drizzle with balsamic vinaigrette.

Nutritional Facts (Per Serving): Calories: 400 | Sugars: 6g | Fat: 22g | Carbs: 12g | Protein: 30g | Fiber: 4g | Sodium: 400mg

Grilled Halloumi and Watermelon Salad

Prep: 15 minutes | Cook: 10 minutes | Serves: 2

Ingredients:

- 8 oz halloumi cheese, sliced (225g)
- 2 cups watermelon, cubed (300g)
- 1 tbsp olive oil (15ml)
- 2 cups mixed greens (100g)
- 1 tbsp balsamic glaze (15ml)
- 1 tsp fresh mint, chopped (5g)
- Salt and pepper to taste

Instructions:

1. Preheat grill to medium-high heat. Brush halloumi slices with olive oil.
2. Grill halloumi for 2-3 minutes per side, until golden brown.
3. In a large bowl, combine watermelon cubes and mixed greens.
4. Arrange grilled halloumi on top of the salad.
5. Drizzle with balsamic glaze, sprinkle with fresh mint, and season with salt and pepper.

Nutritional Facts (Per Serving): Calories: 400 | Sugars: 10g | Fat: 24g | Carbs: 15g | Protein: 22g | Fiber: 3g | Sodium: 800mg

Grilled Greek Chicken Salad with Tzatziki

Prep: 20 minutes | Cook: 15 minutes | Serves: 2

Ingredients:

- 2 boneless, skinless chicken breasts (200g each)
- 1 tbsp olive oil (15ml)
- 1 tsp dried oregano (5g)
- Juice of 1 lemon (50ml)
- Salt and pepper to taste
- 4 cups mixed greens (200g)
- 1 cucumber, diced (200g)
- 1 cup cherry tomatoes, halved (150g)
- 1/4 red onion, thinly sliced (30g)
- 1/4 cup Kalamata olives (50g)
- 1/2 cup crumbled feta cheese (100g)
- 1/2 cup tzatziki sauce (120ml)

Instructions:

1.Prcheat grill to medium-high heat. Rub chicken breasts with olive oil, oregano, lemon juice, salt, and pepper.

2. Grill chicken for 6-7 minutes per side, until cooked through. Let rest 5 minutes, then slice.

3. Combine mixed greens, cucumber, cherry tomatoes, red onion, and Kalamata olives in a bowl.

4. Top salad with sliced chicken and crumbled feta cheese.

5. Serve with tzatziki sauce on the side.

Nutritional Facts (Per Serving): Calories: 400 | Sugars: 5g | Fat: 22g | Carbs: 10g | Protein: 35g | Fiber: 4g | Sodium: 800mg

Grilled Turkey and Cranberry Salad

Prep: 15 minutes | Cook: 10 minutes | Serves: 2

Ingredients:

- 8 oz turkey breast, sliced (225g)
- 1 tbsp olive oil (15ml)
- Salt and pepper to taste
- 4 cups mixed salad greens (200g)
- 1/4 cup dried cranberries (30g)
- 1/4 cup chopped walnuts (30g)
- 1/2 cup crumbled goat cheese (100g)
- 2 tbsp balsamic vinaigrette (30ml)

Instructions:

Preheat grill to medium-high heat. Rub turkey slices with olive oil, salt, and pepper.

2. Grill turkey for 4-5 minutes on each side, until fully cooked.

3. In a large bowl, combine salad greens, dried cranberries, walnuts, and crumbled goat cheese.

4. Slice grilled turkey and place on top of the salad.

5. Drizzle with balsamic vinaigrette and toss gently.

Nutritional Facts (Per Serving): Calories: 400 | Sugars: 10g | Fat: 20g | Carbs: 20g | Protein: 25g | Fiber: 3g | Sodium: 400mg

Grilled Flank Steak and Arugula Salad

Prep: 20 minutes | Cook: 10 minutes | Serves: 2

Ingredients:

- 8 oz flank steak (225g)
- 1 tbsp olive oil (15ml)
- Salt and pepper to taste
- 4 cups arugula (120g)
- 1/2 cup cherry tomatoes, halved (75g))
- 1/4 red onion, thinly sliced (30g)
- 1/4 cup shaved Parmesan cheese (30g)
- 2 tbsp balsamic vinaigrette (30ml)

Instructions:

1. Preheat grill to medium-high heat. Rub flank steak with olive oil, salt, and pepper.
2. Grill flank steak for 4-5 minutes per side, until desired doneness. Let rest for 5 minutes before slicing.
3. In a large bowl, combine arugula, cherry tomatoes, and red onion.
4. Top salad with sliced steak and shaved Parmesan cheese.
5. Drizzle with balsamic vinaigrette and toss gently.

Nutritional Facts (Per Serving): Calories: 400 | Sugars: 4g | Fat: 25g | Carbs: 10g | Protein: 30g | Fiber: 2g | Sodium: 500mg

Grilled BBQ Chicken Salad with Corn and Black Beans

Prep: 15 minutes | Cook: 20 minutes | Serves: 2

Ingredients:

- 2 boneless, skinless chicken breasts (200g each)
- 1/4 cup BBQ sauce (60ml)
- 1 tbsp olive oil (15ml)
- Salt and pepper to taste
- 4 cups mixed salad greens (200g)
- 1/2 cup corn kernels (75g)
- 1/2 cup black beans, rinsed and drained (75g)
- 1/2 cup cherry tomatoes, halved (75g)
- 1/4 red onion, thinly sliced (30g)
- 2 tbsp ranch dressing (30ml)

Instructions:

1. Preheat grill to medium-high heat. Rub chicken breasts with olive oil, salt, and pepper. Brush with BBQ sauce.
2. Grill chicken for 6-7 minutes per side, until fully cooked. Let rest for 5 minutes before slicing.
3. In a large bowl, combine salad greens, corn, black beans, cherry tomatoes, and red onion.
4. Top salad with sliced grilled chicken.
5. Drizzle with ranch dressing and toss gently. Serve immediately.

Nutritional Facts (Per Serving): Calories: 400 | Sugars: 10g | Fat: 15g | Carbs: 30g | Protein: 30g | Fiber: 8g | Sodium: 600mg

CHAPTER 19: DINNER: Grilled Vegetables and Plant-Based Dishes

Grilled Cauliflower Steaks with Romesco Sauce

Prep: 15 minutes | Cook: 20 minutes | Serves: 2

Ingredients:

- 1 large cauliflower, sliced into steaks (500g)
- 2 tbsp olive oil (30ml)
- Salt and pepper to taste
- 1/2 cup roasted red peppers (120g)
- 1/4 cup almonds (35g)
- 1 clove garlic (3g)
- 1 tbsp red wine vinegar (15ml)
- 1 tsp smoked paprika (5g)
- 1/4 cup olive oil (60ml)

Instructions:

1. Preheat grill to medium-high heat. Brush cauliflower steaks with olive oil, salt, and pepper.
2. Grill cauliflower steaks for 8-10 minutes per side, until tender and slightly charred.
3. In a blender, combine roasted red peppers, almonds, garlic, red wine vinegar, smoked paprika, and 1/4 cup olive oil. Blend until smooth.
4. Serve grilled cauliflower steaks with a generous dollop of Romesco sauce on top.

Nutritional Facts (Per Serving): Calories: 400 | Sugars: 6g | Fat: 32g | Carbs: 22g | Protein: 9g | Fiber: 10g | Sodium: 300mg

Grilled Ratatouille

Prep: 15 minutes | Cook: 20 minutes | Serves: 2

Ingredients:

- 1 medium eggplant, sliced (250g)
- 1 zucchini, sliced (150g)
- 1 red bell pepper, sliced (150g)
- 1 yellow bell pepper, sliced (150g)
- 1 red onion, sliced (150g)
- 2 tbsp olive oil (30ml)
- 2 cloves garlic, minced (6g)
- 1 tsp dried thyme (5g)
- 1 tsp dried oregano (5g)
- Salt and pepper to taste
- 1 tbsp balsamic vinegar (15ml)
- 2 tbsp chopped fresh basil (10g)

Instructions:

1. Preheat grill to medium-high heat. Toss eggplant, zucchini, bell peppers, and red onion with olive oil, garlic, thyme, oregano, salt, and pepper.
2. Grill vegetables for 10-12 minutes, turning occasionally, until tender and slightly charred.
3. Transfer grilled vegetables to a large bowl, and drizzle with balsamic vinegar.
4. Toss gently to combine, and garnish with chopped fresh basil. Serve immediately.

Nutritional Facts (Per Serving): Calories: 400 | Sugars: 12g | Fat: 18g | Carbs: 55g | Protein: 8g | Fiber: 16g | Sodium: 400mg

Grilled Butternut Squash and Kale Salad

Prep: 15 minutes | Cook: 20 minutes | Serves: 2

Ingredients:

- 2 cups butternut squash, cubed (300g)
- 1 tbsp olive oil (15ml)
- Salt and pepper to taste
- 4 cups kale, chopped (120g)
- 1/4 cup dried cranberries (30g)
- 1/4 cup chopped walnuts (30g)
- 2 tbsp crumbled feta cheese (30g)
- 2 tbsp balsamic vinaigrette (30ml)

Instructions:

1. Preheat grill to medium-high heat. Toss butternut squash cubes with olive oil, salt, and pepper.
2. Grill squash for 10-12 minutes, turning occasionally, until tender and slightly charred.
3. In a large bowl, combine kale, dried cranberries, and chopped walnuts.
4. Add grilled butternut squash to the salad and toss gently.
5. Top with crumbled feta cheese and drizzle with balsamic vinaigrette. Serve immediately.

Nutritional Facts (Per Serving): Calories: 400 | Sugars: 12g | Fat: 20g | Carbs: 45g | Protein: 8g | Fiber: 8g | Sodium: 300mg

Grilled Zucchini Rolls with Goat Cheese

Prep: 15 minutes | Cook: 10 minutes | Serves: 2

Ingredients:

- 2 medium zucchinis, thinly sliced lengthwise (300g)
- 2 tbsp olive oil (30ml)
- Salt and pepper to taste
- 4 oz goat cheese (115g)
- 1 tbsp fresh basil, chopped (15g)
- 1 tbsp fresh chives, chopped (15g)
- 1 tsp lemon zest (5g)

Instructions:

1. Preheat grill to medium-high heat. Brush zucchini slices with olive oil, and season with salt and pepper.
2. Grill zucchini for 2-3 minutes per side, until tender and grill marks appear. Let cool slightly.
3. In a bowl, mix goat cheese, basil, chives, and lemon zest until well combined.
4. Spread a thin layer of the goat cheese mixture on each zucchini slice and roll up tightly.
5. Secure with a toothpick if needed and serve immediately.

Nutritional Facts (Per Serving): Calories: 400 | Sugars: 5g | Fat: 30g | Carbs: 12g | Protein: 15g | Fiber: 4g | Sodium: 400mg

Grilled Vegetable Wrap with Hummus

Prep: 15 minutes | Cook: 10 minutes | Serves: 2

Ingredients:

- 1 medium zucchini, sliced lengthwise (150g)
- 1 red bell pepper, sliced (150g)
- 1 yellow bell pepper, sliced (150g)
- 1 red onion, sliced (150g)
- 2 tbsp olive oil (30ml)
- Salt and pepper to taste
- 4 whole wheat tortillas (240g)
- 1/2 cup hummus (120g)
- 1 cup baby spinach (30g)

Instructions:

1. Preheat grill to medium-high heat. Toss zucchini, bell peppers, and red onion with olive oil, salt, and pepper.
2. Grill vegetables for 8-10 minutes, turning occasionally, until tender and slightly charred.
3. Spread a thin layer of hummus on each tortilla.
4. Divide grilled vegetables and baby spinach evenly among the tortillas.
5. Roll up the tortillas tightly and serve immediately.

Nutritional Facts (Per Serving): Calories: 400 | Sugars: 8g | Fat: 16g | Carbs: 55g | Protein: 10g | Fiber: 12g | Sodium: 600mg

Grilled Stuffed Tomatoes with Rice and Herbs

Prep: 15 minutes | Cook: 20 minutes | Serves: 2

Ingredients:

- 4 large tomatoes (800g)
- 1 cup cooked rice (200g)
- 2 tbsp olive oil (30ml)
- 2 cloves garlic, minced (6g)
- 1/4 cup chopped fresh parsley (15g)
- 1/4 cup chopped fresh basil (15g)
- 2 tbsp grated Parmesan cheese (15g)
- Salt and pepper to taste

Instructions:

1. Preheat grill to medium-high heat. Cut the tops off the tomatoes and scoop out the insides. Set aside.
2. In a bowl, mix cooked rice, olive oil, garlic, parsley, basil, Parmesan cheese, salt, and pepper.
3. Stuff the tomatoes with the rice mixture.
4. Place stuffed tomatoes on the grill and cook for 10-12 minutes, until tomatoes are tender and the filling is heated through.
5. Serve immediately.

Nutritional Facts (Per Serving): Calories: 400 | Sugars: 10g | Fat: 18g | Carbs: 50g | Protein: 8g | Fiber: 5g | Sodium: 300mg

Grilled Salmon with Dill Yogurt Sauce

Prep: 15 minutes | Cook: 20 minutes | Serves: 2

Ingredients:

- 2 salmon fillets (300g each)
- Juice and zest of 1 lemon (50ml, 5g)
- 2 tbsp olive oil (30ml)
- Salt and pepper to taste
- 1 cup plain Greek yogurt (240g)
- 1 tbsp fresh dill, chopped (15g)
- 1 clove garlic, minced (3g)
- 1 tsp lemon juice (5ml)

Instructions:

1. Marinate salmon fillets in lemon juice, lemon zest, olive oil, salt, and pepper for 10 minutes.
2. Preheat grill to medium heat. Grill salmon for 4-5 minutes per side, until cooked through.
3. In a small bowl, mix Greek yogurt, fresh dill, minced garlic, and lemon juice to make the dill yogurt sauce.
4. Serve grilled salmon with a dollop of dill yogurt sauce on top.

Nutritional Facts (Per Serving): Calories: 400 | Sugars: 4g | Fat: 20g | Carbs: 5g | Protein: 50g | Fiber: 0g | Sodium: 400mg

Grilled Shrimp Skewers with Lemon Garlic Butter

Prep: 15 minutes | Cook: 10 minutes | Serves: 2

Ingredients:

- 1 lb large shrimp, peeled and deveined (450g)
- 2 tbsp olive oil (30ml)
- 3 cloves garlic, minced (9g)
- Juice and zest of 1 lemon (50ml, 5g)
- Salt and pepper to taste
- 1/4 cup melted butter (60ml)
- 1 tbsp chopped fresh parsley (15g)

Instructions:

1. Preheat grill to medium-high heat. Toss shrimp with olive oil, garlic, lemon juice, lemon zest, salt, and pepper.
2. Thread shrimp onto skewers.
3. Grill shrimp skewers for 2-3 minutes per side, until shrimp are opaque and cooked through.
4. In a small bowl, mix melted butter with chopped parsley.
5. Drizzle grilled shrimp with lemon garlic butter before serving.

Nutritional Facts (Per Serving): Calories: 400 | Sugars: 1g | Fat: 25g | Carbs: 2g | Protein: 35g | Fiber: 0g | Sodium: 800mg

Grilled Tuna Steaks with Avocado Salsa

Prep:15 minutes | Cook: 10 minutes | Serves: 2

Ingredients:

- 2 tuna steaks (200g each)
- 2 tbsp olive oil (30ml)
- Salt and pepper to taste
- 1 avocado, diced (150g)
- 1 small red onion, finely chopped (50g)
- 1 small tomato, diced (100g)
- Juice of 1 lime (30ml)
- 1 tbsp fresh cilantro, chopped (15g)

Instructions:

1. Preheat grill to medium-high heat. Brush tuna steaks with olive oil and season with salt and pepper.
2. Grill tuna steaks for 2-3 minutes per side for medium-rare, or until desired doneness.
3. In a bowl, combine diced avocado, red onion, tomato, lime juice, and chopped cilantro to make the avocado salsa.
4. Serve grilled tuna steaks topped with avocado salsa.

Nutritional Facts (Per Serving): Calories: 400 | Sugars: 2g | Fat: 25g | Carbs: 10g | Protein: 35g | Fiber: 7g | Sodium: 300mg

Grilled Swordfish with Pineapple Salsa

Prep: 15 minutes | Cook: 10 minutes | Serves: 2

Ingredients:

- 2 swordfish steaks (200g each)
- 2 tbsp olive oil (30ml)
- Salt and pepper to taste
- 1 cup pineapple, diced (150g)
- 1/2 small red onion, finely chopped (50g)
- 1 small red bell pepper, diced (100g)
- Juice of 1 lime (30ml)
- 1 tbsp fresh cilantro, chopped (15g)

Instructions:

1. Preheat grill to medium-high heat. Brush swordfish steaks with olive oil and season with salt and pepper.
2. Grill swordfish steaks for 4-5 minutes per side, until cooked through.
3. In a bowl, combine diced pineapple, red onion, red bell pepper, lime juice, and chopped cilantro to make the pineapple salsa.
4. Serve grilled swordfish steaks topped with pineapple salsa.

Nutritional Facts (Per Serving): Calories: 400 | Sugars: 10g | Fat: 20g | Carbs: 20g | Protein: 35g | Fiber: 4g | Sodium: 300mg

Grilled Halibut with Tomato Basil Relish

Prep: 15 minutes | Cook: 10 minutes | Serves: 2

Ingredients:

- 2 halibut fillets (200g each)
- 1 tbsp olive oil (15ml)
- Salt and pepper to taste
- 2 large tomatoes, diced (300g)
- 1/4 cup fresh basil, chopped (15g)
- 1 tbsp balsamic vinegar (15ml)
- 1 clove garlic, minced

Instructions:

1. Preheat grill to medium-high heat.
2. Brush halibut fillets with olive oil and season with salt and pepper.
3. Grill halibut for 4-5 minutes per side until opaque and cooked through.
4. In a bowl, combine tomatoes, basil, balsamic vinegar, and garlic. Season with salt and pepper.
5. Serve the grilled halibut topped with tomato basil relish.

Nutritional Facts (Per Serving): Calories: 400 | Sugars: 4g | Fat: 15g | Carbs: 8g | Protein: 50g | Fiber: 2g | Sodium: 300mg

Grilled Mahi-Mahi Tacos with Mango Slaw

Prep: 20 minutes | Cook: 10 minutes | Serves: 2

Ingredients:

- 2 mahi-mahi fillets (200g each)
- 1 tbsp olive oil (15ml)
- Salt and pepper to taste
- 1/2 tsp chili powder (2g)
- 4 small corn tortillas (60g each)
- 1 cup shredded cabbage (100g)
- 1 tbsp lime juice (15ml)
- 1 mango, julienned (200g)
- 1/4 cup red onion, thinly sliced (30g)
- 2 tbsp fresh cilantro, chopped (10g)
- 1 tbsp low carb sweetener (12g)

Instructions:

1. Preheat grill to medium-high heat.
2. Brush mahi-mahi with olive oil, season with salt, pepper, and chili powder.
3. Grill mahi-mahi for 4-5 minutes per side.
Warm tortillas on the grill for 1-2 minutes per side.
4. Mix cabbage, mango, red onion, cilantro, lime juice, and sweetener in a bowl.
5. Flake mahi-mahi, divide among tortillas, and top with mango slaw.

Nutritional Facts (Per Serving): Calories: 400 | Sugars: 10g | Fat: 12g | Carbs: 40g | Protein: 28g | Fiber: 8g | Sodium: 300mg

Grilled Seafood Paella

Prep: 20 minutes | Cook: 30 minutes | Serves: 2

Ingredients:

- 1/2 cup Arborio rice (100g)
- 1 tbsp olive oil (15ml)
- 1/2 onion, finely chopped (50g)
- 1 clove garlic, minced (3g)
- 1/2 red bell pepper, chopped (75g)
- 1/2 green bell pepper, chopped (75g)
- 1 cup chicken broth (240ml)
- 1/2 cup white wine (120ml)
- 6 large shrimp, peeled and deveined (150g)
- 6 mussels, cleaned (150g)
- 1/2 cup peas (75g)
- 1/4 tsp saffron threads (1g)
- Salt and pepper to taste
- 1 lemon, cut into wedges (100g)
- 2 tbsp fresh parsley, chopped (10g)

Instructions:

1. Preheat grill to medium-high heat. Heat olive oil in a large, grill-safe skillet. Add onion, garlic, red and green bell peppers, and cook until softened.
2. Stir in Arborio rice, coating well with oil and vegetables. Add chicken broth, white wine, saffron threads, salt, and pepper.
3. Place skillet on grill, close lid, and cook for 15-20 minutes, stirring occasionally, until rice is tender.
4. Add shrimp, mussels, and peas to the skillet. Cook for another 5-7 minutes, until shrimp are opaque and mussels open.

5. Remove from grill, garnish with lemon wedges and fresh parsley. Serve immediately.

Nutritional Facts (Per Serving): Calories: 400 | Sugars: 5g | Fat: 15g | Carbs: 45g | Protein: 25g | Fiber: 5g | Sodium: 600mg

Grilled Steak Fajitas with Guacamole

Prep: 15 minutes | Cook: 20 minutes | Serves: 2

Ingredients:

- 8 oz flank steak (225g)
- 2 tbsp olive oil (30ml)
- 1 tbsp lime juice (15ml)
- 1 tsp chili powder (5g)
- 1/2 tsp cumin (2.5g)
- Salt and pepper to taste
- 1 red bell pepper, sliced (150g)
- 1 green bell pepper, sliced (150g)
- 1/2 red onion, sliced (50g)
- 4 small flour tortillas (120g)
- 1 avocado, mashed (150g)
- 1 tbsp lime juice (15ml)
- 1 tbsp fresh cilantro, chopped (15g)
- Salt to taste

Instructions:

1. Preheat grill to medium-high heat. Marinate flank steak in olive oil, lime juice, chili powder, cumin, salt, and pepper for 10 minutes.
2. Grill steak for 4-5 minutes per side, until desired doneness. Let rest for 5 minutes, then slice thinly.
3. Grill bell peppers and onion for 5-7 minutes, until tender and slightly charred.
4. In a bowl, mix mashed avocado, lime juice, cilantro, and salt to make guacamole.

5. Warm tortillas on the grill for about 1 minute per side.

6. Assemble fajitas by placing steak, grilled vegetables, and guacamole on tortillas.

Nutritional Facts (Per Serving): Calories: 400 | Sugars: 5g | Fat: 20g | Carbs: 35g | Protein: 25g | Fiber: 6g | Sodium: 600mg

Grilled Vegetable Lasagna

3. In a skillet, sauté onion and garlic in olive oil until softened, about 5 minutes.

4. In a bowl, mix ricotta cheese with dried basil, dried oregano, salt, and pepper.

5. In a greased baking dish, layer grilled vegetables, ricotta mixture, marinara sauce, and mozzarella cheese. Repeat layers, ending with a layer of marinara and a sprinkle of Parmesan cheese on top.

6. Cover with foil and bake at 375°F (190°C) for 30 minutes. Remove foil and bake for an additional 10 minutes until cheese is bubbly and golden.

7. Let lasagna rest for 10 minutes before serving.

Nutritional Facts (Per Serving): Calories: 400 | Sugars: 10g | Fat: 22g | Carbs: 30g | Protein: 20g | Fiber: 8g | Sodium: 800mg

Prep: 25 minutes | Cook: 50 minutes | Serves: 4

Ingredients:

- 2 zucchini, thinly sliced (2 zucchini, 400g)
- 1 eggplant, thinly sliced (1 eggplant, 300g)
- 2 bell peppers, sliced (2 bell peppers, 300g)
- 1 onion, finely chopped (1 onion, 150g)
- 3 cloves garlic, minced (3 cloves garlic, 15g)
- 2 cups ricotta cheese (2 cups, 500g)
- 2 cups marinara sauce (2 cups, 500ml)
- 2 cups shredded mozzarella cheese (2 cups, 200g)
- 1 cup grated Parmesan cheese (1 cup, 100g)
- 1 tsp dried basil (1 tsp, 2g)
- 1 tsp dried oregano (1 tsp, 2g)
- Salt and pepper to taste
- Olive oil for grilling and greasing

Instructions:

1. Preheat grill to medium-high heat.

2. Brush zucchini, eggplant, and bell peppers with olive oil. Grill until tender, about 4-5 minutes per side. Set aside.

CHAPTER 22: BONUSES

Your Ultimate Grocery Shopping Guide

To maximize your grilling adventures, we've crafted a 30-day grocery shopping guide specifically. This guide streamlines meal preparation by prioritizing fresh, natural ingredients and reducing reliance on processed foods. Pay attention to hidden sugars in sauces and marinades. Adjust quantities as needed, embracing the grill's ability to enhance the flavors of whole foods. Relish the journey of preparing healthy, delicious meals with your grill! Enjoy the culinary adventure!

Grocery Shopping List for 7-Day Meal Plan

Proteins

Eggs (for Grilled Breakfast Burrito with Eggs and Chorizo, Grilled Breakfast Flatbread, Grilled Breakfast Quesadilla, Grilled Pancakes, Grilled Cinnamon Rolls, Grilled English Muffin, Grilled Bacon and Egg Breakfast Sandwich)
Chorizo (for Grilled Breakfast Burrito)
Ribeye Steak (for Grilled Ribeye Steak)
Chicken Breasts (for Grilled Lemon Herb Chicken Breasts, Grilled BBQ Chicken Thighs)
Portobello Mushrooms (for Grilled Portobello Mushroom Burger)
Pork Tenderloin (for Grilled Pork Tenderloin Salad)
Bacon (for Grilled Breakfast Flatbread, Grilled Breakfast Quesadilla, Grilled Bacon and Egg Breakfast Sandwich)
Baby Back Ribs (for Grilled Baby Back Ribs)

Salmon (for Grilled Salmon)
Shrimp (for Grilled Shrimp Skewers)
Pork Chops (for Grilled Pork Chops)
Tuna Steaks (for Grilled Tuna Steaks)
Spicy Turkey Sausage (for Grilled Spicy Turkey Sausage)
Halibut (for Grilled Halibut)
Ground Beef (for Classic Grilled Cheeseburger)

Dairy and Dairy Alternatives:

Cream Cheese (for Grilled Stuffed Jalapeños, Grilled Cinnamon Rolls)
Mozzarella Cheese (for Grilled Portobello Mushroom Burger)
Swiss Cheese (for Grilled Portobello Mushroom Burger)
Feta Cheese (for Grilled Pork Tenderloin Salad)
Butter (for Grilled Breakfast Flatbread, Grilled Pancakes, Grilled Cinnamon Rolls)
Greek Yogurt (for Grilled Salmon with Dill Yogurt Sauce)

Fruits:

Apples (for Grilled Pork Tenderloin Salad)

Mango (for Grilled Avocado and Mango Salsa)
Lemons (for Grilled Lemon Herb Chicken Breasts, Grilled Shrimp Skewers)
Berries (for Grilled Pancakes)
Avocados (for Grilled Avocado Halves with Salsa, Grilled Avocado and Mango Salsa)

Vegetables & Herbs:

Mixed Salad Greens (for Grilled Pork Tenderloin Salad)
Spinach (for Sautéed Spinach, Grilled Pork Chops)
Rosemary (for Grilled Ribeye Steak)
Potatoes (for Rosemary Potatoes)
Jalapeños (for Grilled Stuffed Jalapeños)
Broccoli (for Grilled Lemon Herb Chicken Breasts)
Bell Peppers (for Grilled Breakfast Burrito, Grilled Spicy Turkey Sausage)
Artichokes (for Grilled Artichoke Hearts)
Cabbage (for Coleslaw)
Cauliflower (for Grilled Cauliflower Steaks)
Tomatoes (for Grilled Avocado Halves, Grilled Avocado and

Mango Salsa, Classic Grilled
Cheeseburger)
Red Onions (for Grilled
Avocado Halves, Grilled
Avocado and Mango Salsa,
Grilled Spicy Turkey Sausage)
Garlic (for various dishes)
Fresh Herbs (parsley, dill, basil
for flavoring and garnish)

Grains & Bakery:

Whole Wheat Tortillas (for
Grilled Breakfast Burrito, Grilled
Breakfast Quesadilla)
Whole Wheat Buns (for Classic
Grilled Cheeseburger)
Pancake Mix (for Grilled
Pancakes)
Cornmeal (for Cornbread)
Breadcrumbs (for various
dishes)

Nuts & Seeds:

Pecans (for Grilled Pork
Tenderloin Salad)

Pantry Staples:

Olive Oil
Balsamic Vinegar (for Grilled
Pork Tenderloin Salad)
Apple Cider Vinegar
Dijon Mustard
BBQ Sauce (
Soy Sauce (for Grilled Flank
Steak)
Spices (salt, pepper, smoked
paprika, cumin, oregano,
thyme, rosemary)
Low Carb Sweeteners
Honey (for various dishes)
Flour (for Grilled Cinnamon
Rolls)
Baking Powder (for Grilled
Pancakes)

Vanilla Extract (for Grilled
Cinnamon Rolls)

Miscellaneous:

Dark Chocolate (for desserts)
Sugar-Free Sweeteners (if
required for desserts)

Grocery Shopping List for 8-14 Day Meal Plan

Proteins

Sausage (for Grilled Breakfast
Skewers, Grilled Breakfast
Pizza)
Beef Tenderloin (for Grilled
Beef Tenderloin)
Eggs (for Grilled Breakfast
Pizza, Grilled Breakfast Tacos,
Grilled Shrimp and Egg Tacos)
Chicken Breasts (for Grilled
Chicken and Vegetable
Skewers, Grilled BBQ Chicken
Salad)
Ground Turkey (for Grilled
Turkey Burgers)
Chorizo (for Grilled Breakfast
Tacos)
Pork Tenderloin (for Grilled
Pork Tenderloin)
Pork Spare Ribs (for Grilled
Spare Ribs)
Turkey Thighs (for Grilled
Turkey Thighs)
Shrimp (for Grilled Shrimp and
Egg Tacos)
Sirloin Steak (for Grilled Sirloin
Steak)
Flank Steak (for Grilled Flank
Steak)
Tilapia (for Grilled Tilapia)

Dairy and Dairy Alternatives:

Feta Cheese (for Grilled Turkey
Burgers)
Parmesan Cheese (for Grilled
Eggplant Parmesan)
Blue Cheese (for Grilled Pear
and Blue Cheese Spread)
Mozzarella Cheese (for Grilled
Breakfast Pizza)
Cheddar Cheese (for BBQ
Bacon Cheeseburger)
Cream Cheese (for Grilled
Lemon Pound Cake, Grilled
Cheesecake)
Halloumi Cheese (for Grilled
Halloumi Cheese with Lemon)
Greek Yogurt (for various
dishes)
Butter (for various dishes)

Fruits:

Lemons (for various dishes)
Limes (for Grilled Shrimp and
Egg Tacos)
Berries (for Grilled Lemon
Pound Cake, Grilled
Cheesecake)
Pears (for Grilled Pear and Blue
Cheese Spread)
Avocados (for Grilled Tilapia
with Mango Salsa, Grilled BBQ
Chicken Salad)
Mango (for Grilled Tilapia with
Mango Salsa)

Vegetables & Herbs:

Mixed Salad Greens (for Grilled
Flank Steak and Arugula Salad,
Grilled BBQ Chicken Salad)
Spinach (for Grilled Mushroom
and Spinach Frittata, Grilled
Turkey Burgers)

Mushrooms (for Grilled Mushroom and Spinach Frittata)
Bell Peppers (for Grilled Breakfast Skewers, Grilled Chicken and Vegetable Skewers)
Potatoes (for Garlic and Herb Roasted Potatoes, Roasted Sweet Potatoes)
Sweet Potatoes (for Grilled Pork Tenderloin)
Eggplants (for Grilled Eggplant Parmesan)
Green Beans (for Grilled Flank Steak)
Asparagus (for Grilled Sirloin Steak)
Carrots (for Grilled Turkey Thighs)
Black Beans (for Grilled Chicken and Black Bean Quesadillas, Grilled BBQ Chicken Salad)
Zucchini (for Grilled Vegetable Lasagna)
Garlic (for various dishes)
Fresh Herbs (parsley, dill, basil, thyme for flavoring and garnish)
Red Onions (for various dishes)
Cherry Tomatoes (for various dishes)
Cabbage (for various dishes)

Grains & Bakery:

Flour Tortillas (for Grilled Breakfast Tacos, Grilled Chicken and Black Bean Quesadillas)
Whole Wheat Buns (for Grilled Turkey Burgers)
Bread (for various dishes)
Basmati Rice (for Grilled Tilapia with Mango Salsa)
Quinoa (for Grilled Chicken and Vegetable Skewers)

Lasagna Noodles (for Grilled Vegetable Lasagna)

Nuts & Seeds:

Pecans (for Grilled Pork Tenderloin Salad)
Pine Nuts (for various dishes)

Pantry Staples:

Olive Oil
Balsamic Vinegar
Apple Cider Vinegar
Dijon Mustard
BBQ Sauce
Soy Sauce
Spices (salt, pepper, smoked paprika, cumin, oregano, thyme, rosemary)
Low Carb Sweeteners (
Honey (for various dishes)
Flour (for various dishes)
Baking Powder (for Grilled Lemon Pound Cake, Grilled Cheesecake)
Vanilla Extract (for Grilled Lemon Pound Cake, Grilled Cheesecake)
Cocoa Powder
Dark Chocolate (for Grilled Coconut Macaroons)

Miscellaneous:

Dark Chocolate (for desserts)
Sugar-Free Sweeteners (if required for desserts)

Grocery Shopping List for 15-21 Day Meal Plan

Proteins:

Pork Sausages (for Grilled Pork Sausage and Egg Tacos, Grilled Pork Sausages with Onions)
Eggs (for Grilled Pork Sausage and Egg Tacos, Grilled Spicy Breakfast Tacos, Grilled Lentil and Quinoa Breakfast Bowl, Grilled Bacon and Egg Salad, Grilled Breakfast Flatbread)
Swordfish (for Grilled Swordfish with Pineapple Salsa)
New York Strip Steak (for Grilled New York Strip)
Chicken Breasts (for Grilled Greek Salad)
Turkey Breast (for Grilled Turkey Breast)
Shrimp (for Grilled Shrimp Skewers)
Pork Loin (for Grilled Pork Loin)
Pork Tenderloin (for Grilled Pork Tenderloin Salad)
Ribeye Steak (for Grilled Ribeye Steak)
Ground Beef (for Classic Grilled Cheeseburger)
Bacon (for Grilled Breakfast Flatbread, Grilled Bacon and Egg Salad)

Dairy and Dairy Alternatives:

Feta Cheese (for Grilled Greek Salad)
Parmesan Cheese (for Grilled Stuffed Tomatoes)
Mozzarella Cheese (for Grilled Breakfast Flatbread)
Cream Cheese (for Grilled Artichoke Spinach Dip)
Greek Yogurt (for Grilled Salmon with Dill Yogurt Sauce)
Butter (for various dishes)

Fruits:

Pineapple (for Grilled Swordfish with Pineapple Salsa)
Lemons (for Grilled Shrimp Skewers)
Blueberries (for Grilled Blueberry Crisp)
Apples (for Grilled Pork Tenderloin Salad)
Mango (for Grilled Avocado and Mango Salsa)
Berries (for Grilled Lemon Pound Cake)
Avocados (for Grilled Avocado Halves, Grilled Avocado and Mango Salsa)

Vegetables & Herbs:

Mixed Salad Greens (for Grilled Pork Tenderloin Salad, Grilled Greek Salad)
Spinach (for Grilled Artichoke Spinach Dip)
Brussels Sprouts (for Roasted Brussels Sprouts)
Zucchini (for Grilled Corn and Zucchini Quesadillas)
Tomatoes (for Grilled Stuffed Tomatoes, Grilled Eggplant and Tomato Stack)
Garlic (for various dishes)
Fresh Herbs (parsley, dill, basil, thyme for flavoring and garnish)
Red Onions (for various dishes)
Green Beans (for Green Bean Almondine)
Carrots (for Grilled Ratatouille)
Eggplant (for Grilled Ratatouille, Grilled Eggplant and Tomato Stack)
Cabbage (for various dishes)
Bell Peppers (for various dishes)

Jalapeños (for Grilled Spicy Breakfast Tacos, Grilled Jalapeño and Lime Hummus)
Corn (for Grilled Corn and Zucchini Quesadillas)
Potatoes (for German Potato Salad, Garlic Butter and Rosemary Potatoes)
Lentils (for Grilled Lentil and Quinoa Breakfast Bowl)
Quinoa (for Grilled Lentil and Quinoa Breakfast Bowl)

Grains & Bakery:

Flour Tortillas (for Grilled Pork Sausage and Egg Tacos, Grilled Corn and Zucchini Quesadillas)
Whole Wheat Buns (for Classic Grilled Cheeseburger)
Bread (for various dishes)
Rice (for Wild Rice Pilaf, Jasmine Rice)
Jasmine Rice (for Grilled Beef and Veggie Stir-Fry)

Nuts & Seeds:

Pecans (for Grilled Pork Tenderloin Salad)
Pine Nuts (for various dishes)

Pantry Staples:

Olive Oil
Balsamic Vinegar
Apple Cider Vinegar
Dijon Mustard
BBQ Sauce (for various dishes)
Soy Sauce (for Grilled Flank Steak)
Spices (salt, pepper, smoked paprika, cumin, oregano, thyme, rosemary)
Low Carb Sweeteners
Honey (for various dishes)

Flour (for various dishes)
Baking Powder (for Grilled Lemon Pound Cake)
Vanilla Extract (for Grilled Lemon Pound Cake)
Cocoa Powder (
Dark Chocolate

Miscellaneous:

Dark Chocolate (for desserts)
Sugar-Free Sweeteners (if required for desserts)

Grocery Shopping List for 22-28 Day Meal Plan

Proteins:

Sausage (for Grilled Breakfast Casserole, Grilled Breakfast Quesadilla, Grilled Breakfast Tacos, Grilled Shrimp and Egg Tacos, Grilled Pork Sausage and Egg Tacos, Grilled Spicy Breakfast Tacos)
Eggs (for Grilled Breakfast Casserole, Grilled Breakfast Quesadilla, Grilled Breakfast Tacos, Grilled Shrimp and Egg Tacos, Grilled Pork Sausage and Egg Tacos, Grilled Spicy Breakfast Tacos)
Pork Chops (for Grilled Pork Chops with Apple Glaze)
Chicken Thighs (for Grilled BBQ Chicken Thighs)
Bacon (for Grilled Breakfast Quesadilla)
Turkey (for Grilled Turkey Meatballs, Grilled Turkey Thighs)
Chorizo (for Grilled Breakfast Tacos)

Baby Back Ribs (for Grilled Baby Back Ribs)
Tuna Steaks (for Grilled Tuna Steaks)
Chicken Breasts (for Grilled Chicken Caesar Salad)
Shrimp (for Grilled Shrimp and Egg Tacos)
Sirloin Steak (for Grilled Sirloin Steak)
Tilapia (for Grilled Tilapia)
Ground Turkey (for Grilled Turkey Meatballs)
Pork Sausages (for Grilled Pork Sausages with Onions)
Portobello Mushrooms (for Grilled Portobello Mushroom Burger)
Halloumi Cheese (for Grilled Halloumi Cheese, Grilled Halloumi and Watermelon Salad)

Dairy and Dairy Alternatives:

Cream Cheese (for Grilled Stuffed Jalapeños)
Swiss Cheese (for Grilled Portobello Mushroom Burger)
Parmesan Cheese (for Grilled Chicken Caesar Salad)
Greek Yogurt (for various dishes)
Butter (for various dishes)

Fruits:

Apples (for Grilled Pork Chops with Apple Glaze)
Watermelon (for Grilled Halloumi and Watermelon Salad)
Blueberries (for Grilled Blueberry Crisp)
Avocados (for Grilled Tuna Steaks with Avocado Salsa)

Mango (for Grilled Tilapia with Mango Salsa)

Vegetables & Herbs:

Mixed Salad Greens (for Grilled Chicken Caesar Salad, Grilled Halloumi and Watermelon Salad)
Spinach (for Sautéed Spinach, Grilled Artichoke Spinach Dip)
Jalapeños (for Grilled Spicy Breakfast Tacos, Grilled Jalapeño and Lime Hummus)
Zucchini (for Grilled Corn and Zucchini Quesadillas)
Tomatoes (for Grilled Tuna Steaks with Avocado Salsa, Grilled Vegetable Wrap with Hummus)
Garlic (for various dishes)
Fresh Herbs (parsley, dill, basil, thyme for flavoring and garnish)
Red Onions (for various dishes)
Green Beans (for Grilled Flank Steak)
Carrots (for Grilled Turkey Thighs)
Bell Peppers (for various dishes)
Corn (for Grilled Corn and Zucchini Quesadillas, Grilled BBQ Chicken Thighs)
Cabbage (for Coleslaw)
Potatoes (for German Potato Salad, Garlic Butter and Rosemary Potatoes)
Spinach (for Grilled Artichoke Spinach Dip)
Asparagus (for Grilled Sirloin Steak)
Artichokes (for Grilled Artichoke Hearts)

Grains & Bakery:

Flour Tortillas (for Grilled

Breakfast Tacos, Grilled Chicken and Black Bean Quesadillas, Grilled Shrimp and Egg Tacos, Grilled Pork Sausage and Egg Tacos)
Whole Wheat Buns (for Grilled Portobello Mushroom Burger)
Bread (for various dishes)
Spaghetti Squash (for Grilled Turkey Meatballs)
Wild Rice (for Grilled Tilapia with Mango Salsa)

Nuts & Seeds:

Sesame Seeds (for various dishes)

Pantry Staples:

Olive Oil
Balsamic Vinegar
Apple Cider Vinegar
Dijon Mustard (
BBQ Sauce
Soy Sauce
Spices (salt, pepper, smoked paprika, cumin, oregano, thyme, rosemary)
Low Carb Sweeteners (
Honey (for various dishes)
Flour (for various dishes)
Baking Powder (for Grilled Lemon Pound Cake, Grilled Blueberry Crisp)
Vanilla Extract (for Grilled Lemon Pound Cake)
Cocoa Powder (for Grilled Coconut Macaroons)
Dark Chocolate

Miscellaneous:

Dark Chocolate (for desserts)
Sugar-Free Sweeteners

Made in United States
Orlando, FL
03 December 2024

54904004R00043